Not Till Then Can the World Know

Replacement Companies of the Fourteenth Iowa Infantry in the Trans-Mississippi

L. Spencer Busch

and

Valentine L. Spawr

Cover by Safeword Author Services

Valentine Spawr image from *A Diary of the Late Rebellion,* Unit Publishing, 1892

Battle of Pleasant Hill from Buffords Print Publishing House (Library of Congress)

Flag bearer from Currier & Ives, 1861 (Library of Congress)

ISBN: 978-1-7347086-1-5

To Aunt Flippy, who must have known I would cherish and share our ancestor's diary when she passed it down to me

When the graves shall open, and the sea give up its dead, and the secrets of all hearts be revealed, then, and not till then, can the world know what the many thousands of brave Iowans engaged in the service of their country have endured on the battle-field, upon the march and in the camp.

—Colonel John Scott, "Thirty-Second Infantry: History of Regiment"

CONTENTS

PREFACE

Thanks to my great-great-grandfather's decision to keep a diary during his first few months as a Civil War soldier, I had the incredible opportunity of getting to know him a century after he died.

When my mother told me her sister had Valentine Spawr's diary and I said I'd like to read it, she thought I'd probably find it boring. It was just about being sick and doing the same thing every day, she said. I wasn't convinced; I was twelve at the time and had just become obsessed with every detail of my family history.

Fifteen or so years later, around 1980, I was surprised to find a package from my aunt in the mail. It contained a small brown book with cardboard covers and faded writing in pencil on lined pages—the diary! I had been corresponding with her about family history, but I never would have dreamed of asking her for this precious heirloom. I was too busy with our toddlers then to do anything with it, but within a few years I found myself sitting at my first personal computer at work. It was the perfect tool for transcribing the diary during quiet periods. I think the writing in it has become even more faded since then, so I'm glad I did not procrastinate any longer.

The diary actually has been transcribed at least three times. Spawr's widow had the original transcribed and published with the title *A Diary of the Late Rebellion* by a local printer in 1892. (My family's branch had a copy, but my aunt did not share that with me.) And in the 1990s I discovered that Chad Spawr, a half second cousin once removed, had transcribed his family's copy of the book and posted it online for a while. Unfortunately, the printer (Unit Publishing Co. of Lexington, Illinois) edited it heavily—correcting the spelling, attempting to correct the grammar, replacing numerals with words, adding words to make complete sentences, substituting words, and rewriting parts of sentences in ways that were minor but unnecessary. In my opinion, some of the changes were made to reflect the transcriber's prejudices. I have added notes to my transcription where the printer removed or replaced words in ways that changed the meaning. The printer also wrote page numbers at the tops of the original diary pages and marked several places in it with black X's. As these are the only edits made in the original journal, I assume the typesetter simply did the editing while setting the type without marking up the pages further.

In my transcription, I tried to follow standard methods while retaining exactly what my ancestor wrote and the way he wrote it. I have not edited his words, but I have formatted the dates consistently, added spaces between entries written at different times of the same day, and made a few "silent" (unmarked) corrections to make the manuscript more readable. For example, I added capitals and periods where Spawr neglected to use them and deleted words he unintentionally repeated. I have retained his spellings, adding "[*sic*]" only where the reader might otherwise suspect a transcription error. I believe some of the misspellings indicate the way he pronounced the words (e.g., "heft" for "height," "furgotten," "geathering"). I have retained Spawr's unconventional, inconsistent capitalization style as much as possible, but it was especially difficult because most of the C's, J's, and S's beginning words seemed to be halfway between lower and upper case. I tried to interpret them consistently. Where I have inserted a vertical arrow on each side of a word or phrase, Spawr (or possibly the printer in 1892) inserted a word or words above or below a line of writing.

Additional comments on the transcription are included in endnotes.

My mother was wrong—I found the diary fascinating. My ancestor was mustered into Company C (a replacement company) of the Fourteenth Iowa Infantry Volunteers in 1863. He did spend some time in the camp hospital with dysentery, and he was not in any battles during the three months in which he kept the diary at Fort Halleck near Columbus, Kentucky. However, Spawr gives us an interesting account of camp life. He listens to rumors, tracks the sick and dying, drills with the color guard, visits friends, checks out the Steamer Ruth disaster, describes how to make a bed out of tree branches, attends a service at a black church, explores the nearby countryside, and witnesses the hanging of escaped slaves who were convicted of murdering a white family.

He reveals all the human complexity and contradictions of his personality. He's curious about everything and follows all the camp gossip. He condemns drinking, profanity, gambling, and taking things that belong to other people. Lying apparently is acceptable to him, though; he seems proud of using several forms of deceit to leave the fort to pick forbidden apples. One day he opines that dangerous heavy artillery service is where conscripted former slaves belong; the next he self-righteously starts reading a book on kindness. He finds the treatment of a man convicted of mutiny "heartrending," but he barely mentions the impending death of one of his children before commenting on the weather in the next sentence. His grammar and spelling are poor, but he is almost poetic at times when he is lonesome and homesick. I recognize some of my own traits in him—I seem to have inherited his aversion to ministers, his desire to do the right thing, his reluctance to use medicine, and his judgment of others!

His motivation for volunteering for the Army is not obvious. It does not seem to be to free the slaves; in fact, his views of the former slaves in his camp can be described only as racist. He does seem to be enthusiastic about fighting for the Union.

The diary ends in September 1863, so I had to use commanders' reports, letters from other soldiers, newspaper articles, and old history books to learn what he and his regiment did in the remaining year of its service. This book is not intended to be a complete history of the Civil War, Army of the Tennessee, Red River Campaign, or any of the battles described. Instead, I've simply tried to write from the point of view of the soldiers of the Fourteenth Iowa, especially its three replacement companies, while providing a little context for the reader.

As I've worked on this project, I've tried to imagine how the man who recorded his thoughts in camp each day felt when he was on the march and in battle the following year. In 1863 he wrote about "a certain spirit of appropriating other persons' things to their own use that is rather disgusting to a man that wants to do what is right"; in February 1864 he was ordered to forage in the countryside where they were marching if he wanted anything to eat. While in camp he opined that "a fight would be hailed by glad voices by the majority of the regiments at this place," wanted to see the "fun" of such a fight, and mentioned the "pleasure" of dying on the field of battle rather than in the garrison. It's hard to believe he still felt that way after fighting at Pleasant Hill and Pilot Knob in the following months.

LSB

RECRUITS WANTED!

FOR THE

FOURTEENTH IOWA INFANTRY.

$40 Paid in Advance, if Accepted!

THE TERM OF ENLISTMENT IS THREE years, unless sooner discharged. Pay from $13 to $22 per month, commencing from date of enlistment, together with rations, good medical attendance, and everything essential to the comfort of recruits.

This is a first rate opportunity to join a good company. Do not wait to be drafted, but volunteer and secure the bounty. Now is the time to serve your country.

For further information apply at the Recruiting office on Main st., one door above Front, Davenport, Iowa.

JOHN W. MATTHEWS, late of 2d Iowa,
M. J. EAGAL,
oct 27-d1w Recruiting Officers.

Davenport (Iowa) Daily Gazette, November 10, 1862.

INTRODUCTION

WE WISH THE BRAVE BOYS A GOOD TIME

A tall, blue-eyed house carpenter was among the recruits who gathered in Davenport on May 2, 1863, to be mustered into Company C of the Fourteenth Iowa Infantry Volunteers.[1]

The twenty-eight-year-old was Valentine L. Spawr, son of early Butler County settlers Peter R. and Elizabeth (Messer) Spawr. Spawr's parents had established their farm just south of Clarksville after moving to Iowa from Hudson, McLean County, Illinois, in 1854. The younger Spawr, however, was a relatively new arrival. He married Irena Margaret Neighbarger in Hudson in the late 1850s, and their first child, Elizabeth, was born there in 1858. Their second daughter, Clara, was born in Bazaar, Chase County, Kansas, in 1859. They moved to Clarksville after Clara's birth and before Ella's in September 1861. (A fourth daughter was born in Iowa later, but no name or record for her has been found.)

---

1. Valentine L. Spawr pension records; Thrift, *Roster and Record,* 777.

Spawr had enlisted October 20, 1862. His reasons were not recorded, but newspaper ads for recruits for Company C emphasized pay, medical care, and other perks along with service to country and avoiding the draft. Perhaps the advance bounty of $25 and a bonus of $2 he received were factors.

The company Spawr joined was actually one of three replacement companies. Colonel William T. Shaw, an Army veteran and Anamosa, Eureka County, businessman, had organized the Fourteenth Iowa at the end of 1861. The original companies A through C, however, were sent to Dakota Territory as soon as they were formed, and eventually they were permanently detached. At the end of 1862, the War Department let the state of Iowa raise three new companies to replace them.[2]

The men of the other companies of the Fourteenth were already well-seasoned veterans, having fought at Fort Donelson and Shiloh early in 1862. After having to surrender at Shiloh, Shaw and some of his men were held as prisoners of war for months. Men of the Fourteenth who escaped capture at Shiloh were added to the "Union Brigade" until they were able to rejoin the regiment, and they fought at Corinth in October

2. Ingersoll, *Iowa and the Rebellion,* 195–199.

1862. This detachment rejoined Shaw and the rest of his men when they were paroled the following month.

Replacement companies A, with seventy men, and B, with seventy-five men, were mustered in October and November 1862, respectively. Recruiters continued trying to refill the last company through the end of 1862 and into the spring of 1863, but they finally mustered in Company C with only fifty men.

Spawr, who was six feet, four inches tall, became a member of the regimental color guard when he was promoted to eighth corporal within the first few weeks. Members of the guard were conspicuous not just because of the waving flags (both the Stars and Stripes and a regimental flag) but also because the tallest men usually were chosen to be in it. Spawr and the other corporals would be responsible for retrieving the flag and carrying it if the sergeant who was the actual color bearer was shot down in battle. Courage was as important as height. The color guard was placed in the center of the line of battle, and soldiers were trained to follow the flag because smoke, noise, and confusion would make directing them any other way nearly impossible. The enemy often aimed their fire at the color bearers and would try to capture the flag to confuse or demoralize the troops following it. If the color guard turned and ran, the rest of the regiment might follow.

After a month of drilling near Davenport, Spawr and Company C headed to Cairo, Illinois, to join the rest of the regiment, according to the Davenport *Daily Democrat and News* June 3 ("Reinforcements").

> This morning the Sucker State took down one hundred men from Post McClellan. In the party were Lieuts. Miles and Stoughton, with fifty men, for Co. C, 14th Iowa Infantry. . . . The soldiers were a fine-looking body of men, and marched along with their well-filled knapsacks as though they were already used to it. They were in the best spirit and cheered as they passed along, in answer to the good wishes expressed by the citizens who witnessed their departure.

At the end of June, the now complete Fourteenth Iowa was sent from Cairo to Fort Halleck, Kentucky, to begin garrison duty and months of extensive drilling. A former Confederate stronghold, the fort sat on a bluff just up the Mississippi River from the town of Columbus.

"We wish the brave boys a safe journey, a good time, and a speedy return to their homes when the war is over," the *News* said.

PART 1

VALENTINE SPAWR DIARY: A FIGHT WOULD BE HAILED BY GLAD VOICES

Valentine Spawr from *A Diary of the Late Rebellion,* Unit Publishing, Lexington, Illinois, 1892.

Valentine L. Spawr
Columbus Ky July 2nd 1863
A Member of Co C 14th
Regtm [*sic*] Iowa Inft Vols

Price [4_ ct?]

If it Should be my luck to meet an untimely death and this Book should fall in the hands of any friend I make a Special request that he will mail it to

Mrs. Irena M. Spawr
Hudson
McClean Co.
Ills

Stating the cause &c of my death

Columbus Ky June 28th 1863

A record of passing events kept by me and recorded each day as they transpire.

Sunday

June 28th. But little of consequence accured today except the calling to of a steamer that attempted to pass the post[3] without calling and they fired a shot across her bow which caused her to houl ↑to↓ and retreat in double quick. It rained to day as it has done every day for weeks and it is very warm betwen Showers. I will give a short discription of our camp. It is situated a half mile up the river from the city of Columbus on a very high hill Said to be two Hindred feet perpendicular from the waters edge. We are camped inside the fortifications that constitute fort Hallack and it is a good work garisoned with between two & three thousand troops.

---

3. Unit Publishing (Lexington, Illinois) repeatedly transcribed "post" as "port" when it published this as *A Diary of the Late Rebellion* in 1892.

Monday

June 29th. Heavy rain this fornoon. Myself & F. S. Smith[4] took a walk this morning and was caught out in the rain and got thuroughly wet. Another steamer attempted to pass post without stopping and our gun called her to in double quick.

Tuesday

June 30th. This the day for grand review of all inft troops at this post. Consequently this forenoon was spent in preperation for the Same. Formed Batallion at 3 oclock P. M. Went 1 ½ miles from the fort to form the Briggade which was to be reviewed by Br[i]gadier General [Alexander] asboth and about the time that the troops formed it commenced raining & blowing and of all the storms it beat all. Rain pored down on the unprotected Soldier in torents.

Wednsday

July 1st. [This date was originally June 31, and either Spawr or the printer wrote over part of it with heavy, dark pencil to change it to July 1st.] It rained again today as usual. We had no

4. Franklin S. Smith, a wagoner, age 22, was mustered into Company C when Spawr was.

batallion drill. The weather remains very warm betwen Showers.

Thursday

July 2nd. To ↑day↓ past without any thing of consequence. I went to the City of Columbus today to See the place. This after noon we drilled 2 ½ hours on batalion drill. It has been reported for Some days that General [Sterling] price is in force only 30 miles from here marching on us to give us battle but is not credited by most of the Soldiers here. Some wish he would come and I would rather fight him here than any other place.

Friday

July 3d. A day of no importance much. We had a good Batalion drill this evening of Some 2 hours and omitted dress perade. Camp is all preperation for the fourth tomorrow. There is to be a grand celebration 1 ½ miles South east of town which us soldiers must[5] partake in. There is a heavy cloud raising in the west tonight. I think that we will get rain tonight. And our tents is not very good protection against rain. To night I rec[eive]d a letter from home and answered the same.

---

5. Unit Publishing replaced this with "we soldiers will" in 1892.

Saturday

July 4th. A forth of July on the Sacred Soil of Kentucky. Bills out for a grand celebration. Soldiers was marched out. Oration from Judge Bullock and others but no diner apeared and the col[onel] of the Wis[consin] 31 Reg[iment] vol[unteer]s told the boys that they was fooled and we will return to camp and make a diner on hard tack and sow belly and invite the poor Starved critters to come and take dinner at camp for we have plenty such as it is and good anuogh what there is of it. We started back to camp about 2 1/2 miles and it was the warmest day I ever seed I think and by the time we got to camp there was not half of the men in ranks. It was so hot that they could not stand it and had to lay down. Some got in at 1 oclock and some not until 4 or 5.

Sunday

July 5th. All quiet today. I went to town this morning Liet Stoughten[6] & I and there was a little excitement this morning. Our mail boat started off and there was a man on board that the detective Suspicioned and they fired the canon

6. Second Lieutenant William Stoughton, age 32, was mustered into Company C when Spawr was.

and brought her back and took the fellow and he proved to be a rebel Col[onel] in disguise.

Mond[ay]

July 6th. All quiet to day. Nothing of note accured. Weather still warm and river still raising very fast.

Tuesday

July 7th. Nothing to day. All qu[i]et until evening. Then we had a light shower of rain.

Wednsday

July 8th. This morning all of the troops was called up in line and offitially reperted that Vicksburgh was taken on the merning of the fourth of July. The Col[onel] Commanding here told all hands that they might celebrate the accasion. That they was exemp from drill on this day and could all go to town without a pass and I am not well anough to go. The boys is pretty much all going and will have a great spree.

To night I see severl men tight strolling through camp[7] and on [*sic*] any other time they would be incarcerated in the military prison.

The boys went to town and nearly cleaned the town out especialy saloons. They tore out every thing brought chairs and every thing you could think of to camp with them.

Thursday

July 9th. All quiet to day. All feel hard after their spree.

Friday

July 10th. All quiet still today. Weather still very warm. I have been very unwell for Somes [*sic*] days and feel worse today. I am at the Hospital to stay. I don't know how long. I have got something like the bloody flux.[8] About ten oclock this AM the drum beat the long rool which calls every man to get ready for battle.

---

7. In the version published in 1892, this was edited to "several men in camp." Apparently the term "tight," meaning "drunk," offended Unit Publishing.

8. Bloody flux, now called dysentery, is an infectious disease causing severe bloody diarrhea, abdominal pain, fever, and other symptoms. It killed more Civil War soldiers than any other cause. http://www.civil-war-facts.com/Interesting-Civil-War-Facts/American-Civil-War-Diseases-Facts.html

It is now 1,oclock [*sic*] and every Officer and man is ready for duty at a moments warning and ordered to remain So. The enemy is reported but a few miles off in conciderable force.

The report now is that the enemy has taken possession of Union City 20 miles back from this place and our men are still ready to go to attact them. The 32nd regament has went on [*sic*] out on the cars[9] and when the train returns our Reg[imen]t expects to go out. If they go tonight or tomorrow I fear I will not be able to go.

10 oclock PM. Again the long rool is beating and the cry fall in fall in from all direction. I suppose it is another scare although there may be danger. I under stand from an officer that ~~that~~ those men is all to be throwed out on guard that the rebels is marching on us. I cant believe it.

Saturday

July 11th. This morning 7 AM Camp all in arms comeing in from guard and going out. There was an officer at the Hospital stating that he wanted every man put on duty at Such a time as this. I see the Scare has not subsided yet. I spoke to Liet Stoughten to accertain the extent of the raid as

9. Railroad.

near as possible and inform me so I can make a note of it. However I was informed that the 4th Mo Cavelry was attacted badly cut up and two Cos taken prisoners.

I Just understood that the 32nd Iowa I?]n]fant[ry] Reg[iment] got back last night bring[ing] with them some 20 wounded soldiers that belongs to the 4 Mo Cav. They was wounded in the Scurmish and the Rebels could not carry them with them and left them. There was also some killed and they buried them.

12 M.[10] Things is rather quiet again but we keep up very heavy guards yet. I heard a few minutes ago that Co[mpany] D 14th was going out on the cars on a scurmish or recanorter [reconnoiter] and hunt up the enemy. If they should be found they must fight or climb for the success[es] that we ↑have had↓ are bound to clean them out all around if we can. Tomorrow is inspection and all hands is cleaning up around their quarters.

3 oclock PM. All quiet but on the look out for the enemy but I think that it will blow off by and by. I must say that I have transgressed my general rule of detesting ministers for our chapl[a]in has visited me twice since I have been in the hospital

---

10. Noon (abbreviation for 12 *meridiem,* or midday).

and seems very sociable and I think he is much of a gentleman and he is not always moralizeing but ever sotiable and kind and interested in a mans welfare. His name I have not learned but on my next interview with him ↑I will↓ and set him down as an exception of ministers.[11] There is only about 10 men in our hospital and I think will all get well. I have only known of one soldiers dying since we have been here.

All still yet at 5 ½ oclock PM. Some pitching horse shoes others laying around but no man officer or private allowed to leave the camp lines. Keep all hands for the contemplated battle which I fear will not come off at this time and if they must be fought I want them to come now while we are ready and looking for them for tomorrw I will be ready to take hold with the boys if no bad luck.

10 Oclock PM. Camp all up roar. The loud Shrill Sound fall in fall in is heard all over [written over

---

11. Frederick F. Kiner of Mount Pleasant, Iowa, Company I, age 27 at enlistment in October 1861. A Church of God minister, he was promoted to regimental chaplain in April 1863. He had served as orderly sergeant until then. The same year he published *One Year's Soldiering: Embracing the Battles of Fort Donelson and Shiloh, and the Capture of Two Hundred Officers and Men of the Fourteenth Iowa Infantry, and Their Confinement Six Months and a Half in Rebel Prisons* under the name F. F. Kiner (Lancaster: E. H. Thomas). Spawr's parents were members of the Church of the United Brethren in Christ, but Spawr's religion, if any, is unknown.

"of"] camp. They are going out to double the pick[written over "q"]et guard. It has been very cool today and cloudy.

Sunday

July 12th. Very cool [heavy "l" written over a different letter, possibly a "k"] this morning and Smoky. All quiet in camp this morning as though there had been no stir atal for the [past] few days. We have not heard the wherebouts of the rebels yet. I think at examination this morning I will get out of the hospital.

8 oclock AM. Examination is over and I am not released from the hosptal but have got to take 3 blue pills this morning and two tonight.

10 oclock AM The cha[p]lain made us his regular visit and read a chapter and prayed with us. I supose he thought that we would die and he would start a spirit of reformation in us which in a proper Sense of the word is very necessary but men in the army seldom think of hereafter I think from apearance. There certainly is more demoralization in the army than I was willing to admit before I was a member of the same. There is a certain spirit of apropriating other persons things to their own use that is rather disgusting to a man that wants to do what is right. I

understood today that General grant parolled all of the prisoners taken at Vicksburgh both officers and men. And we will probly have to fight them ↑at↓ Some other place.

4 oclock PM. It is very cool today. A man wants a good thick coat to be comfortable. There was another man brought into the hospital to day from our reg[imen]t who is very sick. I understand that we are to be paid off the first of the week. Our chaplin preaches this after noon at head quarters the first time that there has been preaching in the Reg[imen]t since I have been with it. Some think that we will have to fight the enemy yet for they are geathering out here in the country but I dont think so myself. Tonight I expect we will have another Scare or allarm and our boys have to stand all night again. Last [replaces a word that was erased] night the boys on picket had four shots fired at them.

Monday

July 13th. 8 Oclock AM. I am still detained in the hospital and 3 big doses of medacine to take today a good portion of which is quinine. I feel very unwell this morning owing probly to the affect of

Calomil I have been taking for the last 24 hours.[12] I have not heard any news of the anticipated attact on our fort ↑this morning↓. I think ↑there↓ was no allarm given last night at least I heard no long rool nor command to fall in. The battle probly is over for some days any how. I see by the morning paper that supposition is that the back bone of the great rebellion is broken. But I fear that there is some fighting to do yet of some conciderable consequence. It is very cool & lowery[13] this morning. I think we will get rain Soon.

4 oclock PM. It is cool dreary and lonesom today. No allarm nor excitement sofar. I was laying on my cot looking out ju[s]t now and seed a half grown Negro, trotting pacing and cantering around an [*sic*] his hands and feet and a man might very easily mistook him for a babboon. It was as natural a position as I ever seed one in and travels as easy and natural as a dog. There is

12. He probably was right. Calomel, although used to treat diarrhea during the war, "caused explosive diarrhea and projectile vomiting which further dehydrated dysentery patients. Calomel and blue mass were also mercury-based drugs that caused extreme salivation, inflamed gums and loose teeth." https://opinionator.blogs.nytimes.com/2012/10/26/brother-against-microbe/

13. "Lowery" means "gloomy." Unit Publishing changed it to "lovely."

a rumor afloat now that there is a probability of our Reg[imen]t being sent to new Mexico on business but I put no confidence in the report. The scare at this place has had some affect on some of the commanding officers of this place for they have been getting reinforcements in the last few days. There has been several Reg[imen]ts arrived here. I understand the drums is beating and the colors out for dress perade for the 31st Wis[consin] Reg[imen]t. Our Reg[imen]t has not been out on dress perad[e] for a week or more nor theirs until tonight and this is grand weather for drilling so cool. The sick I think is on the increase if any thing in our Reg[imen]t. We have one man in our Reg[imen]t at this hospital by the name of graves[14] belonging [to] Co B that has had the chronic diareah for some time but I think that he is not long for this world any more and some two or three more that is pretty sick. Just now I see an Ambulance come into camp with three or four Ladies wives of soldiers or rather officers of the Wis[consin] Reg[imen]t I see by their going to or among their camps. There is one or two of the Wis[consin] drafted men in our hospital at this time.

---

14. Cyrus B. Graves of Anamosa, Iowa, age 38, Company B.

Tuesday

July 14th. 6 oclock AM. Last night at midnight the camp was all called out again I heard but dont know what the scare was but I understand that our co[mpany] was ordered to report at quarters in the city for instruction or orders. A strang[e] time of night to call troops that distance to receive orders. The rest of the co[mpanie]s I presume was posted on guard out side the fort for I dont see but few men in camp this morning. The cavelry Reg[iment] about a mile from here keeps their horses saddled all the time read[y] to either fight or run I dont know which. I think to run for I dont put but little confidence in their valor. The fourth MO [Missouri]. I have just learned the cause of the afright last ↑night↓. There was a negro came staving[15] at the rates [*sic*] of ten knots per hour stating that there was 15,000 rebels only 3 miles from the fort and would be on us and we asleep and such an ecitement. All hands a fort this morning for fight. I will try and leave the hospital this morning so I can see the fun of some of their reverses and victorys.

8 oclock AM. Been examined. Doctor Says that I may go to my quarters if I would prefer and I Shal go certain but have got to take a pocket full

---

15. An archaic definition of "stave" is to walk or move rapidly.

of quinine with me but quinine is getting very scarce in this country and can hardly be got and so I shal not say any thing seeing it is scarce.

I am now at my quarters now and taken my first ↑dose↓ of medacine for today and understand by scared men that the woods is full of rebels and they sent us ~~forth~~ word that they would be in to try us on. It was announced this forenoon that there would be inspection today. We have fit up and waited until 3 oclock and no inspection yet. I hear great talk today about strenghening the fortifications at the city digging rifle pits &c.

7,oclock [*sic*] PM. All still only all expectation of an excitement tonight. We have Just had our repast of bread coffee & fat meat generally Called among ↑Soldiers↓ Sow belly. I forgot to state that this morning we had a fine shower of rain and prospects looks favorable this evening for more rain. We have had no drill in our Reg[imen]t for some time and now our Lie[u]t[enant] Col[onel] being sick I dont know when we will drill again and then we are harased so much on account of this scare that there is nothing else thought of by the officers and every thing more thought of by the privates. I believe that a fight would be hailed by glad voices by the majority of the Reg[imen]ts at this place. This evening at rool call we withe

the rest of the troops at this place [were ordered?] to lay on their arms and not take off any of their clothes and be ready for any immergency at a moments warning.

Wednsday

July 15th. The night past off and no excitement. We was not called out for any duty. The ↑weather↓ is somewhat ~~cooler~~ warmer but quite pleasant yet. Alaxander March & Edward glen was over to see us this morning. They (or the 32nd is camped out side the fort) [*sic*].[16] They told me that Mr Hayden a son in law of Lie[u]t[enant] Converse was buried yesterday and there ~~th~~ was another man by the name of Smith from their Co[mpany] they thought would die bifore many days. Some of our boys was out through the lines today and got some blackberries which is just now in thier [*sic*] prime. They also got a nice lot of apples which is getting nice now. This appears to bee a fine country for fruit both wild and tame for papaws is plenty and they tell me that grapes plums and parcimmons is in a bundance here. The word came today that Port Hudson was taken by our forces which if confurmed tomorrow will bring forth a thundering national Salute from

---

16. It is not clear whether the parentheses in the diary were inserted by Spawr or by Unit Publishing in 1892.

our batery of iron monsters and it will be given with a will for that will give us possession of the whole Miss River and be a death stroke to the rebellion. I heard a rumor today (and only a rumor) that three Co[mpanie]s from our Reg[imen]t [lowercase "r" written over with capital "R"] our Co[mpany] included will be sent out to Clinton tomorrow which is some ten miles distant from this place. There was about ten or fifteen men detailed this morning to ↑dig↓ a sink on the river bank for privat use of the soldiers and at about two oclock this PM they came to some hard substance that proved to be the very chain that the Rebels had to blockade the river at this place which many will remember reading about.[17] For a short discription of the same I would say that it is made out of about 3 inch round Iron links probly 10 or 12 inches long. The length of the chain no person can tell any thing about. It once reached a cross the river which is near a mile in width and it comes to the top of this hill two hundred feet above the level of the

---

17. The anchor and part of the chain are displayed at the Columbus-Belmont (Kentucky) State Park. "Chain Blockade. The chain stretched across the river by the rebels at Columbus, Kentucky, is controlled by a steam engine on the Kentucky shore, which tightens or loosens it at pleasure. To the bottom of the chain is attached three large torpedoes intended to explode on concussion with the wheel of a boat." *Janesville (Wisconsin) Daily Gazette,* January 10, 1862.

river and is buried ~~I~~in the bank but how far I could not say. They dug down on it and it runs on through the sink it buried of course for the purpose of making it fast at this end. It then run down the bank and across the river being supported accasionly by laying across flat boats and its monstrous weight and the slight working of the flat boat which supported it for they was anchered in the stream and the water is tolerable swift at that place finally wore through the [boats?] and cut them in ["n" written over illegible letter] t[w]o and it was so heavy that its weight broke it. It also as I understand it was hung full of torpedoes and the chain would stop the fleet and the torpedoes could be exploded and destroy the whole thing but it availed them nothing. Some of our boys was over to see the battle ground of Bellmont[18] which is direcly across the river from here and in plane view of this place. I want to go over and take view of it as I have never had to [*sic*] pleasure of being on a battle field. We expect to have to go out on duty for I see some of them think that there is rebels in the country and there may be.

18. Belmont, Missouri, November 1861.

Thursday

July 16th. The night passed off without any allarm. We have just dispatched our very plain breakfast and rec[eive]d an order to detail 8 men and 1 searge[n]t for guard. Prospects look favorable for a fine day. It [is] quite cool this morning. I rec[eive]d a letter from my wife last night written at Hudson Ill[inoi]s[19] stating that she arived at that place on the 14th Inst.

Some of the boys was out to an orchard today and got some apples and some black berries. I think that the present excitement is about over for there is not much said about it today. I was over to the hospital today to see the sick boys at that place that I got acquainted with at that place when I was there sick [the word "there" erased here]. No boys there from our co[mpany] at this time. It has got quite warm today and the soldiers is mostly laying in their tents some writing some cleaning their guns some reading some few playing on their violins. At least one man that I was unlucky anough to get my tent in rather close proximity to that of his for me to get out of the squeak of that miserable instrument for any lenght [*sic*] of time. He is a man that belongs to

19. Spawr and his wife, Irena Margaret Neighbarger, came from Hudson before settling in Iowa. She still had relatives there.

Co[mpany] K. I dont know his name nor do I wish to. And then there is Some I See that is playing on a more favorable soldiers instrument Called Euchre.[20] You will once and a while see a negro strolling through our camp. We have negro cooks mostly.

10,oclock [*sic*] PM. Tonight all is ecitement in the fort. The report is that there is a heavy force marching on us. Our teams is all under whip halling our rations inside the fort from town. I go to bed expecting to be called out before morning.

Friday

July 17th. 6 oclock AM. Morning has came and no allarm given. We are all awaiting our humble repast and the teams is still at work and has been all night halling provisions inside the fortifications. It is plainly to be seen that some of the head officers expect an attact but I am still of the impression that there will be no fight at presant. I see by the morning paper that rumor of the capture of port hudson is confirmed. It surrendered with 12,000 prisoners. They made an unconditional surrender on the 8 inst at 10 oclock AM. I took a prisoner to day for the first [time] since I have been in the service. It was not a

20. Card game.

Secesh. Some calls them boddy guards but in the Service they are generally known as gray backs. Any how I put him to death between [last three letters written over illegible letters] my two thumb nails. The word just came that the Rebels has taken mound City Ill[inoi]s a small place seven miles above Cairo on the Ohio River. There was no troops there to speak of if any atal but I presume that they got a pretty good houl of plunder with concicrable [considerable?] ammunition and I also understand that there was some Secesh[21] prisoners quartered there but dont know the particulars yet. To Judge from appearance I think we will get some rain tonight.

Sa[t]urday

July 18th. 7 oclock AM. All quiet this morning and the night passed of[f] withouout [*sic*] any unusual excitement. I want to go out today and get some buries as I have not been out side of the breast work for over a week. By some cause or another our mail boat did not come down last night.

5 oclock PM. I have taken a good tramp in the Country to day. I started at 8 am and got to camp 3 1/2 PM. I got a nice lot of berries and apples. I

21. Unit Publishing changed this to "rebels" in 1892.

probly walked 15 miles and not being very strong after my brash [rash?] of sickness I was quite week. Concequently I am very tired tonight. The report of the capture of Charlston by our forces reached this place this after noon. However it wants Conformation yet. It looks like rain this evening. It is clowdy. Concequently all of the soldiers[22] out at their several amusements some pitching horse shoes and some one thing and some another and the squeak of that miserable old fiddle is yet free for all to hear wheather they want to or not. I can hear distant fireing this evening from some place that they have got artilery either for a saloot or something else. Seargent Roberts[23] was my companion today in my rambles and I think he is about as tired as myself.

Sunday

July 19th. Today we have Co[mpany] inspection. It is now 8 oclock AM. The guards are falling in now before my tent and also there is a couple of regimints falling [in] a few rods from here for the purpose of going out on a scout.

22. Unit Publishing changed this to "boys" in 1892.

23. Fifth Sergeant Myron L. Roberts, of Delaware, Iowa, age 26. Mustered into Company C when Spawr was.

10 oclock AM. Inspection is over and we have got back to our respective tents and the officers is going around now Seeing how many rounds of cartrages each man has got. I think they are preparing for another battle probly the ↑same↓ as the one we just past through. It is clowdy today but quite warm occasionly sprinkling rain. All qui[e]t today in regard to fighting.

5 oclock PM. I have just returned from hearing a sermon from our chaplin. He preach[ed] a very good Sermon of about one hour. The ↑text↓ was as follows. Man shal not live on bread alone but on every word that proceedeth out of the mouth of god. I have fugotten where you can find it. There was a death in our hospital today. The diseased [*sic*] was a Jerman belonging to Co[mpany] H 14th Reg[imen]t. His name I have furgotten.[24] This evening is warm but clowdy and looks as though we would get rain before morning. We have one man in the hospital with a geathering[25] on the side of his neck. It will go pretty hard with him I think.

We have just been to supper and a very plain one it was as usual. The mail has came and I had some hopes of getting a letter from my family but

24. Probably Edgar Dykeman of Company G.

25. A "gathering" is a pus-filled swelling.

only hoped and was disapointed. I now stop writing to day. The gun will fire in a minute or two and it is within a few rods of our tent and it deafens me every eveng if I am standing stiff and careless.

It just fired clouding the air with smoke and sending its murderous echoe for miles along the river and timber. I would state here for the edification of the reader that every morning at sunrise and every evening at sun-down they fire a large siege[26] gun that stands a few rods from my tent.

Monday

July 20th. All qu[i]et this Morning at 7 PM [*sic*] a good deal of quarling about guard duty. All thinks that they are doing more than their share. I got a pass and went out to the teamsters quarters which is about a half mile out side the fortifications.

9 oclock AM. The prcession have just started to bury the man that died yesterday and the roll of the muffled drums as they beat the dead march sounds rather desolate and the soldiers as they file past at a reverse arms all with their heads

26. Unit Publishing transcribed this as "sized" in 1892.

down marching to the slow time of the music. All and all it is rather a solemn sight.

12 oclock M. All is qu[i]et in camp at this hour. The ambulance and prcession has returned from the funeral. There is a heavy detail for fatigue duty today. They are at work on our breast works.[27] Dress perade was ordered this evening for the first time for some two weeks but was postponed on account of the Lie[u]t[enant] Col[onel] being ordered to move his head quarters away from the breast works which is thought by the commanders would be an obstruction in time of an engagement.

6 oclock PM. There is a very heavy cloud in the north this evening and it looks as though we would have a very heavy storm. It is the first time that we have had the apearance of a wind and rain storm. It thunders quite heavy. I will now close up my days writing for it is getting quite dark and the storm will be on us in a short time. It is all preperation through camp fixing their tents for the aproching storm.

---

27. "Fatigue duty" is a military term for work that does not involve weapons or fighting. The breastworks, or earthworks, are preserved at the Columbus-Belmont (Kentucky) State Park.

Tuesday

July 21st. Last night at dark it commenced raining quite slow and steady and kept it up for 1/2 or 3/4 of an hour when the storm came and it blowed and rained in a most terific manner for 1 1/2 or 2 hours I think. I never seed it blow or rain harder. One Co[mpany] from our Reg[imen]t and one or two Co[mpanie]s [started to write "R..." and wrote over it] from the 31st Wis[consin] Reg[iment] went out on a scout this morning how far or in what direction I dont know. I was over to head quarters and the field battery there was filling up their Caisons with shell ready for an attact which I think they will wait for some time before they see it for I cant fix it up in my mind that the enemy is in any force in this part of the country. I went over to the chaplains quarters by his request and he presented me with two nice little books and one paper. This after noon I seed two men swim across the river and back. It is said to be one mile in width at this place.

It is now night pleasant and cool and the boys is enjoying a free rassle three or four rods from my tent. I went over to the 31st Wis[consin] Reg[imen]t this evening to make a visit to Major [William J.?] Gibson major of that Reg[imen]t. I seed him the fourth of July and recognized him as an old acquaintance from Black River Wis[consin].

Wednsday

July 22nd. This day has past quiet. Quite cool last night and this morning. But very warm later in the day. We had batallion drill this evening rather short but spirited. Our Co[mpany] was ordered to town tonight as Co[mpany] guards. There is two full Co[mpanies] goes every night. The sun set beautiful and is pleasant.

Thursday

July 23d. 2 oclock PM. It is very warm today. Last night after our boys went out on guard and the few of us that was left at camp went to bed the tents and napsacks of those that was on guard was nearly all over hawled by some one and a great many articles of clothing taken. I was over to the hospital today to see the sick and find them all in tolerable good fix excep Graves which I have before spoken of as being very sick at the same time I was at the hospital. He I think has but few hours or days at most to live. He is turning purple all over his stomach and bouels today. The seargeant was called in by the stewart to see him while I was in there but I did not hear what the doctor said of him. There was one man went to the hospital from our company L H Winchell[28] from Shellrock. Things generally is rather quiet here today. No excitement atal for some days now. Our news from ↑the↓ army still remain flatering. I am sitting in what I call our shcool [*sic*] house a large shade made of brush and poles for the purpose of us uncommitioned officers reciting our lesson to the Col[onel] every day at 3 oclock PM it is quite cool under here but our cloth tents is the warmest things when the sun shines that I ever Seed for a man to stay in.

It is now quite dark. We had batallion drill this evening after which I eat supper and came out to the same shade that I writ in today and have been reading ever since until it got to dark to see. Some is pitching horse shoes some playing cards but I have not pitched a shoe or played a card since I have been at the place nor dont expect to.

10 oclock PM.[29] I resume my task of writing. I have been reading by a candle until my eyes aches and I will retire now for the night. Tomorrow we have got to go to studying and reciteing tactics that is us uncommitioned officers. I feel very unwell tonight and have felt so

---

28. Lyford H. Winchell, age 18, was mustered when Spawr was.
29. Version published in 1892 transcribed time as "12 o'clock p.m."

for several days but am trying to wear it out without taking medacine.

Friday

July 24th. It is now morning and rather nice and cool although it is agoing to be very warm today. We had Co[mpany] drill before breakfast this mor[n]ing of about an hour.

9 oclock AM. I have repaired to my shade. It is quite warm a ready this morning but has the apearance of clouding up. The white fleecy clouds is floating between us and the clear blue Sky and makes a beautiful and pictuesque Scenery such as we dont see every day. The air Sweet Soft and balmy. Our adgutant was telling me this morning that the rebels was conscripting men only five miles from this place and I see that they are getting another Scare up for it is ordered that no man shal go out side the picket guard witout a pass from the prvost marshal and they have got a Cav[alry] patroll out all of the time to pick up the ~~guards~~ boys that runs the guard. I rec[eive]d a visit this morning from Jacob Hickle Austin Wilcox and George Sonash and they have just left me and gone back to their Reg[imen]t. Our boys is getting very impatient about their money which they should had July 1st. I still feel quite unwill. I feel as though I would be sick if I would give up.

It is now 8 oclock PM.[30] I see a group of men starting from the 31st Wis[consin] Reg[imen]t hospital at a reverse arms marching to the slow time of the dead march which to plain↑ly↓ ↑tells↓ a sad story for they were accompanied by an ambulance with the American flag thrown over a box that says in here is the remains of a poor soldier that could not even have the pleasure of expiring on the field of battle mid the din and roar of canon and Small armes. It was anounced this morning that this afternoon we would have inspection ~~this~~ ~~evening~~ which done away with batallion drill and all hands has been cleaning up their clothes and guns and quarters for the event. At this time it looks as though we would have rain tonight. From the front of my tent where I now sit I can see some six or eight miles down the river. I can now see a steamer coming up that I hope may have Some news from the South. Boats is very plenty here and some very large ones. We have strong expectations of peace here now quite soon god Send it. It is now dark and I have lit the candle. We had inspection this evening which went off Satisfactoral I think.

30. Transcribed as "3 o'clock p.m." in version published in 1892.

Saturday

July 25th. 8 oclock AM. Quite cool this morning but some muddy on account of a very heavy rain we had last night. It came up about 10 or 12 oclock with a vengance and oh horrors but it did blow and rain. I got Some wet which left me with a very Sore throat and feeling rather uncomfortable on account of the same. I think that I will confine myself principally to writing today. I would Say I went to the Hospital this morning as usual to see how the Sick is getting along for our Co[mpany] has two men in the Hospital neither one dangerous though I think. I found them all in tolerable good fix except poor Graves of whome I have before spoken of as being incurable I thought. And sure anough there lay his inanimate clay. He departed this life last night. Today he will be buried. Deaths are [written over erased word that might be "is"] becoming more frequent here now.

12 oclock PM.[31] Graves was burried this fore noon.[32] I was out reading under my regular shade that I have before spoken of and heard the dead march playing on a band and went to the breast

---

31. Transcribed as "Two o'clock p.m." in version published in 1892.

32. His body later was moved to the National Cemetery, Mound City, Illinois, Section C, grave 3084.

works which is right by and looked over to the grave yard which is ~~which~~ in plain view and only about a half mile distant. There I See them consigning another soldier to the tombs according to order by the honors of war. It must be quite a help to a mans feelings to know that if he dies in the army that he will be escorted to his grave by a martial band and 16 Soldiers at revers arms which is not used on any other occasion and then have 32 guns fired over his grave. The funeral that is just going off I suppose to belong to the 32nd Reg[imen]t as it did not go out of the fort. Things is generally pretty quiet today about camp. I have just got word that our quarters will be inspected this evening.

4 [o'cl]ock PM. For want of past time I will take my pencil and write a few words again. At about this time in the evening if there is any time that the mind of a man will soar back to its native home and there greet and comune with those loved ones that is far far away it is in the evening espetially in camp where he will here and see all kinds of foolery and I must say hear all kinds of wicked↑ness↓ and vulgar language but I do believe that it will be a school of ~~mora...~~ moralization to me or almost any other man that ever calculates to be any thing after they leave the Service for they will become disgusted with

wickedness blasphemy and vulgarity. It looks as though it would rain again tonight but I hope it may not.

Sunday

July 26th. 10 oclock AM. This is another beautiful Sabbath morning although quite warm in the sun but I have retreated to my regular shade and feel quite comfortable so far as heat is concerned. I went over to the hospital and seed the sick and found them all on the mend. I then gave the chaplain a call and found him as sotiable and clever as usual. He informs me that there will be preaching at 4 oclock this PM under the Shade I am now writing under. We are getting no news of any concequence from below now for some cause. I feel some better this morning in boddy than I have for a week or more but I have a gloomy moody feelling that has been hanging around me for some cause for weeks past. They say that the reason that I dont partake in their gambols and sports is because the chaplain and me is So farmiliar and I am under conviction but I know better for I know that any man of a meditative mind seperated from family and home will have gloomy spells attact him. I will lay down my pencil and ↑read↓ in ~~the life of~~ a book I have been reading for some time entitled life and trials of

David Copperfield[33] until dinner is called and will probly write some more after dinner.

It is now 4 oclock PM. Our mail boat just past camp and all are waiting for our Chaplain to bring up ["with" inserted and then erased] the mail. I have hopes that I will get a mail tonight. I have not had one for Some time.

I just went over to chaplains but got no mail and we will have no more mail until Tuesday. This is another one of those calm Sarine evenings that will bring all of the old and pleasant assosiations back to a mans mind that ever attended his life and then as [if] to taunt him will harrow up all of the misteps and blunders of his life all rushing with an over whilming mass on his mind to make him opbrade him self.

Our chaplain has made a grand disapointmt this evening. It is now six oclock and he has not preached which he proposed to do at four. I dont know wheather he lied or not. I think so.

Monday

July 27th. 7 oclock AM. We have just came off of Co drill and waiting for breakfast. I will write a

33. Unit Publishing changed this to "Life and Death of David Copperfield."

few moments again. I had an invitation by our chaplain last night to go to darkey church. We got there and the black women come in such a rush that we thought that we would be under trod. We kept giving our seats and finaly I concluded to leave the house So out we goes. By the way the man that was in the pulpit requests the chaplain to Stop with ↑him↓ and chaplain request me to stop also but I refused and went out to get fresh air and stopped at the window. The man in the pulpit was a captain in the 32nd Iowa Reg[imen]t quartered at this place delivered a Sermon or something of the kind from Sec[ond] Corinthians 2nd Chapt[er] 1st verse and after the sermon commenced I heard Some one reading a text around at the door on the out side of the house and it atracted my attention for it read as follows (although at a supressed tone) you damned black son of a bitch. I thought I would step around the corner and See them comment on it which was soon done by cuffey No two bringing a stunny blow down on top of his head that sounded like striking a rock with a club and it was briskly returned by cuffee No one and so on until No two thought he had argued long anough in that way and would try some other and says John dont you strike me again and so on and was finally parted by other darkeys after a good deal of disturbance out doores and but little inside. Finally the sermon was over and a spirited exortation from our chaplain Mr. Kiner. He finally got out and we came back to Camp all right. And I feel all right except ["ion of" erased] a cold I took by going to sleep naked after going to bed very warm and have a bad head ache this morning and think that I am Satisfied with darkey meeting. I understand from the chaplain that [there] is a probability of us getting our pay in a few days now. I trust it may be so. This by the way is a very pleasant day beautiful and clear and not So warm as usual. I think that this after noon I will take a stroll out of the fort for the purpose of getting some brush to put on my bedstead which would be quite a curiosity to some old fogy that never slept without his featherbead. It is constructed by driving four forks in the ground and putting two poles on them ans↑w↓ering for the side rails to your bed stead. You then take Short poles and lay across them close togeather. If you dont put them close at the end of the week you will wish you had done so. You then take one blanket lay on the poles lay your self on the blanket and take your other blanket and lay over you.

8 oclock PM. The day is past and gone. The evenings Shades appear and they appear most beautiful calm and lovely. We had nice dress perade this evening. The brass band belonging to

the 31st Reg[imen]t Wis[consin] vol[unteer]s was reduced to the ranks this evening for refusing to play at a funeral of one of their Reg[imen]t that was buried today. There was a young man recovered this morning that was drowned day before yesterday. He raised when the morning gun fired. There is one Com[manding] ["and" erased] officer and ten ↑men↓ to be detailed out of our Reg[imen]t to guard a Co[mpany] of deserters that is in the prison of this place. The deserters belongs to an Ill[inois] Reg[iment]t. They are to start them down to Island No. 10[34] tonight some time. The guards are to take four days rations with them.

Tuesday

July 28th. 7 oclock AM. This is a beautiful morning cool and pleasant. There was seven companies detailed from this post last night to start this morning to diferant points in country for some purpose I dont know what nor dont know how long they will remain. The Lie[u]t[enant] of the picket was shot through the arm last night when on duty by some one in ambush. His wound not dangerous I think. The dastardly act was committed about midnight. Just now as I was writing I heard the boys hollowing [hollering] like

34. An island on the Mississippi south of Columbus.

mad Saying it is coming right hear. I looked out of my tent and seen a furious whirlwind. It was right ["It was right" was smaller than the text on the rest of the page as if the word "right" was used originally and then erased and replaced with "It was right"] above my tent some 3 rods that is the heft[35] of it. The second tent above me was stript of papers loose clothes and every thing almost [the word "almost" is a different size, is written with different pencil, and has a period after it as if the printer in 1892 erased a word and replaced it] late news papers and all. They sent some men out to pick up papers letters &c.

There was a funeral this evening. He was a member of the 31st Reg[imen]t Wis[consin] Vol[unteer]s and five minutes before his death got up [to] eat and thought he was better.

Wednesday

July 29th. 7 oclock AM. This morning is quite cool. We have very cool nights here for some time past. There was another death in the 31st Wis[consin] hospital. They seem to be unlucky. We have but few men in our hospital and they are appearantly all on the mend but a poor fellow that gets into their hospital (which is always full)

35. The main part of it? An archaic meaning of "heft" is "bulk."

if he gets out he most generally goes in a box feet first.[36]

Teamster F. Smith was over to my quarters this morning and I went over with him to his quarters a half mile out side the fort and took dinner. Had a good sing[37] and came back to see a mammoth pole raised a pole that cost $150 that is the work [word?]. They got it nearly up and the rope broke and down went pole and mashed all to pieces fur it was very heavy 2 ½ feet at but[t]. Worked out 8 square and 80 ft long being only one Section or one half as they was raising it in two pieses. They are agoing to go to work in the morning to get out another. This evening there was another death in the 31st hospital.

Thursday

July 30th. This forenoon was a little cloudy but quite warm and it is now 10 oclock and we are Signing the pay rool and this evening or tomorrow we will get our money and then I will

36. This paragraph implies there was more than one hospital. The house at the Belmont-Columbus State Park may not be the one used by the Fourteenth Iowa.

37. In an affidavit for Spawr's widow's pension application July 22, 1884, Myron Roberts remembered "his being a good singer" and that he "used to sing a great deal for the boys."

feel better about my family when they get the money.

It is now about 5 oclock PM. We had a very heavy Shower of rain this evening and it has just Stopped raining but Still thunders heavy and I think we may get Some more rain tonight. We got some pay today for the first as a regular payday since we have been in the service. I see a good many soldiers has obtained passes and others have went with out them and gone to town.

We had a very disagreeable sight this evening. The ↑troops↓ of this place was all called out in 3 batallions forming two long lines two ranks each at about ["of" erased] thirty ↑paces↓from each other and there was a man by the name of raney from some Indianna Reg[imen]t marched through that was aprehended as a deserter down in arkansas. He had a large play card fastened on his back with deserter printed on it. He had to march to the tune of the rouges [rogue's?] march played by our Reg[imen]tal band. He was quite lame having to be shot through the leg before they catched [illegible erasure] him. He also was sentanced to forfeit all pay due or here after due and put in prison at alton [Illinois] during the war.

Friday

July 31st. This has been a very warm day. This morning I went to town and expressed 60$ home to my wife.[38] This afternoon I got my likeness taken and Sent to my wife.[39] Also this afternoon there was two Co[mpanie]s from our Reg[imen]t ours included and two co[mpanie]s from the 31st Wis[consin] Reg[imen]t to go out to Union City with one days rations distant 20 or 25 miles. They got about half way and heard there was conciderable force of rebels at union City and turned round and came back in 2 or 3 hours for they went on the cars. I could not get to go Seeing the Regimental Colors did not go for I am a member of the color guards.

Saturday

Aug 1st. This morning I took a trip to town to see what might be seen. While there there was a boat loaded with soldiers (that was mustered out of the service) and they fired a blank ["et" erased] cartrage to call her to. She refused to come or at least went a head and we fired a gain and brought her to and in a short time there was a gun boat came up towing a wreck that been all

38. About three months' pay.

39. No photographs of Spawr have been found.

riddled to pieces and probly taken from the rebels. They say they are fighting down at Hickman 15 miles from here. There has been some firing in that direction and this morning at two oclock there was some Inf[an]t[ry] and some Cav[alry] started down there. We will probly get word tonight from there. I understand that our Colors have got back. They have been off to St. Louis for the purpose of being printed.[40] The name of the state Reg[imen]t and name [*sic*] of battles they have been through which is Donaldson and Shiloe.

Sunday

Aug 2nd. 7 oclock AM. This Sabbath again the regular day for inspection and all hands is at work cleaning up brass guns clothes buttons and shoes and I suppose we will have preaching this afternoon. I guess that the Hickman battle of yesterday was more imagination than real for I could hear no firing that sounded like an engagement nor can hear nothing from it. Concequently I dont think there was any thing of it.

40. The original diary clearly says "printed," not "painted," although regimental flags were painted.

5 oclock PM. There was a lot of men detailed today to be ready at a moments worning with 2 days rations to go off some place not known of course by them selves or any one else nor wont be until they get to their destination. It is no part of a soldiers business where he is a going so he is ready when called for and finds out where he is going after he gets there. I took a walk today out side the fort probly ↑a↓ half mile. Got under the Shade of a tree and took a rest and then returned by the way of the 32nd Reg[imen]t and got in about 4 oclock.

Monday

Aug 3d. 7 oclock AM. It is quite pleasant this morning. Some what clowdy and look as though we would get rain. The detailed men has left camp. Part of them left yesterday evening in the fore part. The remainder started at ten oclock last night. I understand that they went to guard the loyal citizens at the State Election which is today and they fear the garillas which is scattered over this country to conciderable extent and of all Swearing and fussing it is [in] camp this morning. Men that came off guard this morning has got to go on piquet guard at 8 oclock this Morning and stand 30 hours more it seem that men can['t?] stand it. It is rather a lucky occurrence for me that I am exempt from duty and I dont know but what I will have to going [*sic*] to help them for I dont think that they can Stand the duty. There is two or three of them that is runing down and appearantly without cause or disease but will soon blow away beyond a doubt. The doctor says they are as able for duty as they will ever be. Our Co[mpany] was not able to fill their call for guards for there was not men anough able for duty to fill the detail. The fort looks as though it was deserted today for the guards has just started out to their posts.

Sundown. The evening gun has just fired and I will close up my days writing. I writ a letter and Sent home today containing a picture of myself. Our reg[imen]t has got So low that we cant raise men anough for dress parade. Health is not very good at this place at present although there is not much fatality at present.

Tuesday

Aug 4th. Pleasant and cool this morning. I payed 25 cts for a half month cooking this morning.

6 oclock PM. It has been very warm today. We still omit dress perade. There was a soldier drowned in the river at this place. He belonged to the 4th Mo [Missouri] Cav[alry] and was under

the influence of liquor[41] and rode his horse in to drink and got off and went down to rise nomore. The mail boat just passes the fort. In an hour we will get our mail brought up by our chaplain.

Wednesday

Aug 5th. Today has been very warm. Last night about 10 oclock the Steamer Ruth a very fine large boat took fire about 6 miles above this place and was consumed[?] in a Short time and a great deal of baggage and property lost with upwards of 400 head of Government beef cattle which was en rout for some point below.[42] I have furgotten the name of the place. They was all lost I understand. No human lives lost that I have heard of. Today about 10 oclock AM the rubbis[h] from the reck was in a gorge at this place and skiffs was thick in the [water] propelled by men that was picking

41. Unit Publishing omitted "drink" and "horse" in 1892.

42. "From the breaking out of the fire up to the time when I jumped overboard was three minutes, and then the fire was bursting from the windows of the office in the front of the boat. Not a soul could have lived five minutes from its commencement. The boat was a new one, and had the most perfect apparatus for subduing fire of any on the Western waters, but so rapid was the progress of the flames that it was impossible to make use of it." From "THE DISASTER ON THE MISSISSIPPI.; Destruction of the Steamer Ruth. From the Philadelphia Inquirer," *New York Times,* August 16, 1863. http://www.nytimes.com/1863/08/16/news/disaster-mississippi-destruction-steamer-ruth-philadelphia-inquirer.html.

up things from the fatal boat. There was a great deal of baggage and things obtained floating that had probly been thrown over board and they say that there was an army paymaster aboard with two millions [*sic*] dollars which was all lost.

Thursday

Aug 6th. It is now 5 oclock PM and has been a very warm day. There was a detail of men went from this place this morning. Acording to the best information that I can get about three hundred in number under command of Lie[u]t[enant Col[onel] [Joseph H.] Newbold of our reg[imen]t. The report came in about noon that they got out [to] Union City and there engaged the enemy and Sent back for reinforcements which was Sint as follows first Kansas batery and all troops here belonging to the regular army probly about one hundred in number. There is a heavy cloud raising very fast which is about over us. I think there is pretty hevy wind with it. The word just came to me as I was writing that there was two of our men killed out at union City and more wounded whe[n] the word left there. I dont believe any thing about it yet. Large drops of rain begins to fall rather Slow yet but I think we will get a good Shower. About an hour ago we were notafied to fit up for inspection that the troops of this place would be inspected by Major Gen [Stephen A.] Hurlbut who was passing this place but the rain begins now to fall in torrents and it is late in the after noon and I think that we will have to omit inspection for we are going to have a very heavy fall of rain. There comes the general for we hear a government dispatch boat whistle and boom boom boom goes the canon for 13 Shots in quick Succession as a salute for the worthy General Hurlbut.

Friday

Aug 7th. It is now evening and it has been pretty warm. There has been nothing of concequence today except a little occurrance which was grand sport for some but[43] was a heart rending Sight for me. It was a man and a young man to belonging to an Ind[iana] reg[imen]t was tried and convicted of mutiny before a court martial and sentenced to be ignominiously discharged from the Service and imprisoned three years at hard labor at Alton prison Ill[inoi]s. Also to be drumed out of camp and through camp the facings to be cut off his clothes in public by an oncommitioned officer and step to the tune of the rougs [rogue's?] march at the point of the bayonets of a strong

43. Unit Publishing edited out "was grand sport for some but" here in 1892.

guard that escorted him. Also two large and rather handsom cards placed one on his back and [erased, illegible word] one on his breast with the word mutiny nicely printed on it so all could read it. All the troops in this vicinity was assemble[d] and arrang[ed] according to order at a charge bayonet. Another funeral in the Wis[consin] reg[imen]t ↑today↓.

Saturday

Aug 8th. It is now evening again and has been very warm today although there has been some conciderable wind a stir. I went to town this morning to get some tape to have my shivalito [chevron to?] put on acording to a spetial order or request made by the Col[onel] Commanding. While I was at town there was four dead men came floating down the river. Some men got skiffs and went out and was getting them out when I left. They was some of the crew of ↑the↓ Ruth that burned the other night. They caught 3 yesterday and 3 early this morning which makes 10 got out at this ↑place↓. It was assertained that there was about 50 persons lost altogeather by that fatal accident. Our batallion was called out this evening and had a Short drill in the manuel of arms in stead of dress perade. The evening is very fine and pleasant as the Sun gets low for there is a pleasant breeze Stiring.

Sunday

Aug 9th. Things has been quite [*sic*] today. No inspection today as usual on Sunday. Preaching at 4 oclock PM by Chaplain Kiner of our Reg[imen]t and a good prctical Sermon it was warning the soldier to be ware and Shun the snares that is Continually Set for them by both men and women. I volunteered to go and post guard at the Railroad tonight and we just soon start. There is 21 men in the squad to guard the depot.

And I went to sleep and would [have] slept all nigh[t] comfortable had it not been for the mosquitoes for I was not needed nor called all night. It will be remembered that I am exempt from duty and [it] was a volunteer act goining [*sic*] on guard.

Monday

Aug 10th. 5 oclock PM. The day past so far with [no?] excitement atal. The soldiers duty at this place is very heavy ↑in↓ our Reg[imen]t. Our Reg[imen]t is on duty every other day both privates and uncommitioned officers which is wearing very fast on the men and the reader may rest asured that there is quarling and grumbling anough to. I writ and Sent two letters to my wife today one of which contained a picture of the author of these lines. I rather presume that we will have dress parade this even and it is near time now. Tonight will be a dull night for me for we get no mail on mondays and I will have nothing to look for and probly it will save me being disapinted as I have been for some evenings past . . . [*sic*]

The day is past and gone. The evening shades apear. Dress parade is over and I am again in my tent pencil and book in hand. The 32nd Reg[imen]t is on dress perade at this moment for I hear their band playing.

Tuesday

Aug 11th. 9 oclock A M. It is very warm already and will ↑be↓ nearly unindurable by two oclock. One man a member of our Co[mpany] Liford winchel starts home this morning on sick furlough for 30 days . . [*sic*][44]

5 oclock PM. I went this morning got F. S. Smith (a teamster detailed from our Co[mpany] and was

44. Private Winchell died of chronic diarrhea November 12, 1863, at home in Shell Rock, Iowa.

an espetial friend and assotiate of mine Since he has been a member of our Co[mpany]) and got permition to go out in the country with 4 men (as I pretended to get some brush to made sheds [shades?]) but the bu[s]iness was to get apples. We came to the orchard and there the guard (for there is a picket post in the orchard) told me that they had orders to let no man get apples more than he wanted to eat. I told him that I wanted to go out on the other road to go back to camp. He ↑said↓ you have a permit I Suppose to bring you[r] Squad out. I told him I had. He let us pass without showing my permit which I did not have. I had [a] permit from our Reg[iment] officers but had to have a written permit from the provost martial to pass the piquet line but once out side I did not care for none of them has any right to stop a soldier from coming in and we drove around [to] the other side of the orchard which is very large. It must be a half mile Square and arithmatic cannot begin to calculate the amount ↑of↓ fruit that is there in that orchard and beatiful fruit to. We then filled our wagon box half ful of apples cut a few brush and throwed on top and started home and crossed the piquet line at another place. For fear some one will acuse me of Jayhawking a thing that I detest I will say that the man that owns this plantation and orchard went South and joined the rebel army and his property was confiscated and there is no one living at or near the place. We then came by a large rebel magazine or a magazine that the rebels had in the bluff and when this fortification fell in our hands our men was and is to this day afraid to open the doors for fear there is a private torp[e]do or match that will by the opening of the doore will ignite the powder in the magazine and they think that it communicates with torpedoes buried all ["of" erased] over the fort and town which undoubtedly is buried here but where they comuncate I could not tell. Today they raised their mommoth flag pole. Got it up without accident got the flag run up to the top and it looked very nice. Its highth I dont know but I think it is as high a one as I ever seen any place.

Wednesday

Aug 12th. 12 oclock M. All quiet today. I have slept most of the forenoon and after waking feel rather lonesom and dull. It is cloudy and cooler than common today. I have looked for a letter until I am discouraged and have no heart to look any more. There was a lake Steamer passed up by this place today. Boats is runing very thick at this place at the presant time.

6 oclock PM. We just came off dress perade. Had a good time. I bore out the glorious old Stars and

Stripes while the band played dixie in their best time.

Thursday

Aug 13th. 9 oclock AM. It is very warm today indeed. There is nothing of any concequence going on at this time. Things is rather dull for some days past. I think that we are agoing to have some very warm weather now from apearance of things. The day passed off quiet but very warm. I went down to town to See if I could See any thing new but there was nothing going on. I came back very much fatigued and we had a good dress perade in a short time after I got to camp. This evening is very fair and pleasant.

Friday

Aug 14th. 7 oclock AM. Quite pleasant this morning. Has some apearance of clowding up. If it does not it will be another very warm day. Our second Lie[u]t[enant][45] is under arrest and confined to his quarters and has been for some days. He probly will be court martialed for this is the second time he has been under arrest for the same offence that absenting him self from camp without permission and drinking and behaveing

45. William Stoughton.

unbecoming. There will be one of our prards [privates?] arrested this morning for being absent or going to town without leve and staying away from dress perade. Our first Lie[u]t[enant][46] tells me he thinks he will be court martialed for he has committed like offence frequently since he has been in our co[mpany].

10 oclock AM. The man that we thought would be court martialed was sentenced by the Col[onel] to go ↑on↓ knapsack drill but I don't know how long he is to drill but he is out drilling with knapsack and blanket on and the Sun shining as hot as it is possible. I can hardly live in the Shade it is so hot.

7 oclock PM. We just came off dress perade and there was a cloud raising fast when perade broke and it has Just commenced raining. I think we will have a wet night and I am Sick tonight with a pain in my bowels and stomach but hope to be better tomorrow.

9 oclock PM. The mail just came in and brought a letter for me from my wife which I was glad to get for I had never heard from the money I Sent nor

46. First Lieutenant Herman A. Miles of Waverly, Iowa, age 37. Mustered into Company C when Spawr was.

heard from my family for some time. I will now go to bed.

Saturday

Aug 15th. 7 ½ oclock AM. They are mounting guard at the presant time and it is a continuel roar of drums and scream of fyfes.[47] I will stop writing now and go and answer the letter I rec[eive]d last night. It is agoing to be very warm today. I feel some better this morning but not well by any means.

2 oclock PM. It has been one of the warmest days I think I ever witnessed until about an hour ago. There was a cloud got up high anough to cover the sun and it was but a short time until it went to raining. I thought as it came up we would have a very heavy rain and wind but it rains very moderate yet and the wind does not blow but it has got nice and cool. I writ ↑my↓ letter today and sent it out.

7 oclock PM. We had a good but mild shower which cleared away in time for dress perade on which occasion we was visited by our new Comander Brig[adier] Gen[eral] [Andrew Jackson] Smith who takes command of this

47. Unit Publishing edited this to "roar of drums and fifes" in 1892.

division instead of Brig[adier] Gen[eral] Asbott [Asboth] who is ordered to take another command ↑at pense[c]ola florida↓.

Sunday

Aug 16th. 9 oclock AM. At this time in the morning it is ↑so↓ warm that a man can hardly get his breath. I fear that Sickness is a going to commit heavy ravages among our soldiers for there is new cases every day although but few deaths but the warm weather to apearance is Just commencing here. I think I am better this morning than I was yesterday although I took a small dose of castor oil last night. Guard duty is so heavy and so few men left in camp when the guard is mounted that regular weekly inspection is again defered as it was last sunday. Teamster Smith came up to the fort this morning to get me to take one of his mules and go out into the Country but I was not able to go so I will stay at my tent and suffer on with heat for there is not a breath of air stirring and the rays of an August ↑Sun↓ in southern Ky seems to go right through one of those cloth tents.

6 oclock PM. We had a good little Shower of rain this after noon that makes it quite pleasant and cooll. We have no dress parade this evening. I

feell very unwell this evening.[48] I fear that I am a going to have the bloody flux again but then I will get along without taking meda[c]ine as long as possible. Our chaplain preached this forenoon in town and this after noon in camp but I did not feel well anough to go and it is almost night and some cloudy but I dont hardly think that it will rain tonight. I think that the Sickness is on the increase in camp now. Diareah mostly.

Monday

[This entry and the following one were scrawled.] Aug 17th. The [day] passed off very still for it was awful hot. I[t] as warm a day as I ever witnessed. Howevar it is a little cooler this evening. We Just got off dress perade. I am very unwell this evening.

Tuesday

Aug 18th. It was very warm to day so warm that a man could not see any satisfaction in any place. I feel very unwell tonight yet so much so that I cant write so I will stop.

48. Unit Publishing omitted this sentence in 1892.

Wednsday

Aug 19th. Very warm today. Omitted dress perade this evening. I feell a very little better tonight. Nothing transpired to day of note. I hear the mail boat whistling and I look for a letter tonight. It looks Some thing like rain tonight. Two or three of our boys has got the ague health. I think that health is better than it was Some time since at least in our Co[mpany]. The army it appears has taken up Summer quarters generally and movements will lay still generally until cool weather.

Thursday

Aug 20th. To day quite warm but cloudy. Nothing occured of concequence. We had general inspection this afternoon.

Friday

Aug 21st. All quiet. Weather very warm. Had inspection tonight. Got no mail last night. All anxious tonight.

Saturday

Aug 22nd. 9 oclock AM. The day commenced with a damp heavy fog. About 8 oclock the fog raised and the Sun came out with awful power. It will nearly wilt a man down under its scorching rays. There is [nothing] transpiring now a days at all.

7 oclock PM. It has been very warm today. Lie[u]t[enant] Miles Seargeant Fisher[49] and myself went to town but stayed a short time and seen nothing worthy of note. We gad [had] good dress perade this evening. I see a band of Contrabands came in camp this eve.[50] I suppose that they will be put right in the Negro Reg[imen]t that is camped some distance out side the fort. It is a new Reg[imen]t Just raising and drilling and they do well drilling better than I was willing to give them cred[it] for. There was 50 rebel soldiers got to our lines today took the oath and a majoraty of them is agoing to enlist in the union army at this place.

Sunday

Aug 23d. Teamster Smith and myself this morning got a pass from the provost martial to pass us out the piquet lines. Took two of his ~~team~~ mules saddled them got on and started for the country in the direction of clinton which is 10 miles from this place. We went 2 ½ miles and

49. Third Sergeant Irving Fisher of Nashua, Iowa, age 25. Mustered into Company C when Spawr was.

50. "Contraband" was the term for an escaped or former slave.

stopped at Judg Bullocks[51] for water. We got a drink and had an invitation to eat some pears which we excepted for they were very ripe and nice. The Judg is a rather portly man of good and almost commanding appearance. His hair quite grey and a very pleasant disposition in all [erasure—could have been a capital "M" as in "Mrs."; see following sentence] and people say that until this portion of the country fell into union hands that he was a rabbid secessionist but he has now taken the oath of illegiance. Mrs. Bullock his wife is a very fine looking and sotiable woman and I think that they both would make good neighbors and I call them good union people for we stopped probly an hour and left after receiving a very corteous good bye and a strong invitation to call again. We went on toward clinton one mile to another farm stopped and got what peaches we wanted to eat offered to pay for them which they refused. He also is a good union man. We went on to the next house and got what cider we could drink for which they refused to take pay all of them saying that if all soldiers would behave as we did they would like to receive visits from them but it pains my heart to say that there is a great many men in the army that thinks that they have licens to commit all kinds of

51. Edward I. Bullock.

deprudations and even thinks it smart. We then went on further got some melons and peaches from a negro and he was the only man during the day that would take pay for any thing. He charged 25 cts for a small mellon and probly 3 doz peaches. We finally started back and got to camp just in time for dress perad[e] which is at six oclock and I am very tired for it has been very warm today.

Monday

Aug 24th. About 10 oclock this AM [the "A" written over a "P"] we got a regular dry storm that beat any thing I ever seed. I was laying in my tent and there was a regular tornado came up from the north and the ground being very dry of all dusts I ever seen it beat all. It lasted about two hours and then calmed down ~~very~~ a little but there is still a stiff gale blowing. After the heft[52] of it was over so a man could navigate I went out in camp to see the affect and it was a hard looking sight a great ma[n]y streets in camp that I could not walk through for brush and tents for they had shades fixed up all over camp pretty much and most of them was blown down and a great many tents also and the air at this time feels almost like snow and getting colder all the time.

52. In the sense of the archaic meaning of "bulk"?

7 oclock PM. It yet blowing hard and the dust blowing and it has got very cold for Aug[ust]. You will See men going around with vest dress coat and over coat on all buttoned up to the chin and then complain of being cold. For my part I have dress coat and vest on and would wear an over coat if I had one here but last spring when we left Iowa for this country I thought probly ["that" erased] we would go into the field and I Sent my over coats home. It is ↑so ↓windy this evening that we have to omit dress perade. This is another class of weather that will make a mans thoughts run back to loved ones at home where he could sit down among the innocent Sports of his children in preferance to the vulgar profane sports of the soldier in camp.

Tuesday

Aug 25th. It has been very cool today and is agoing to be a cool night. All has passed off quiet today. I walked to town this morning but seed nothing but a town full of soldiers mostly on guard for there is a great many guards kept there. This afternoon there was about fifty more contrabands came in and was examined by the Seargeant. A great many of them did not want to be excepted made all kinds of excuses claiming to be unhealthy. One Said he had had the congestive chills for 9 months at a stretch.

Wednsday

Aug 26th. The [day] has passed off rather quiet. Lie[u]t[enant] Stoughtens trial by court martial commenced today in columbus. Dress perade is just over and our ~~days~~ work is done for today. I took a walk out of the fort today. It has [been] very pleasant today. Cold anough for frost this morning quite warm at noon a[nd] cool anough to be pleasant tonight.

Thursday

Aug 27th. It was quite warm from 10 oclock until evening but was cold anough this morning ↑and↓ tonight there is a heavy cloud raising in the west and distant thunder is quite frequent. I fear that we will get rain tonight. I feell lonely and desolate this evening. I have looked for a letter every night for a week and got none and am about discouraged looking. The trial of Lie[u]t[enant] Stoughten is still progressing slowly. I think that it will take a week for them to get through. There was a dispatch came to day said to be official that Stated that fort Sumpter had Surrendered to Gen [Quincy Adams] gilmore. I hope it may be so. We had dress perade this evening which was good and spirited.

Friday

Aug 28th. It has been warm anough to be pleasant and to warm. I went to town to visit the military prison today. There is about 150 rebel prisoners in there some eight or ten captains about the Same number of Lieut[enant]s and two or three Col[onel]s. There was 150 of them taken up the river early this morning destination Chicago. We just came off dress perade and it is a beautiful pleasant evening. It seemes as though nature was smiling on us through the evening twilight and the moons broad Smiling face is Just apearing above the eastern horizon. The trial of our Lieut[enant] is Still in progress. By some cause we did not get our mail last night. I have some hopes that I will get a letter tonight. I have not had one from my wife for 2 weeks.

Saturday

Aug 29th. Quite cool today. Last night about ½ past 9 oclock we was all at once visitted by one more of them dry tornadoes a teriffic wind and the air filled with dust and blowed for one hour and filled every thing with dust. This morning I seen at sunrise that there was Several tents down yet. I rec[eive]d a letter today from my wife stating that her and my two oldest children was well but the two youngest was very sick. The babe she fears will not get well.[53] This is beautiful weather today clear and nice. The air feels like autumn. The trial of Lieut[enant] Stoughten is still in progress. I have not been to town today and have heard nothing from the trial only that they was still in progress. I writ a letter to my wife today. As we came in off dress perade there was about 30 more negroes came in to the hospital head quarters for examination. Some comes in every few days in Squads of 30 to 50. They are conscripted. Mind they are not Vol[unteer]s. However some of them is very willing to go into the army but according to my knouledge the majority of them plays off or trys to. The blacks that they are taking in at this place is for heavy artilery service. [54] Very good service I think for them. The evening gun has just fired which says plainly it is night.

Sunday

Aug 30th. The day has been pleasant very cool in the morning and quite warm in the middle of the

53. Spawr does not mention this child again nor has any other record been found of its existence or death.

54. Fourth U.S. Heavy Artillery Colored.

day. I have spent the day So far laying around camp although I dont know but I may take a stroll this evening late. I went over to see the Chaplain and got a book out of our library entitled the affects of Kindness a very fit subject for camp reading. I went over to the hospital and found the Sick mostly on the mend. We have three men in there now one of which is pretty sick and he asked me to take his pocket book and keep it for him until he gets well or Starts home on sick furlough which he expects to do next week if he is able to travel. I dont think he will ever get strong again. The chaplain tells me he will preach for us this evening at 4 oclock.

7 oclock PM. We had a good sermon at 4 and a good dress perade at six and there was a man in Co H fainted in ranks fell and was helped off the perad[e] ground. I have not heard from him since. This evening qute cool. The sun just set and looked as red as a ball of fire as ↑it↓ set in a bright golden horizon which is very frequently seen in this country on summer evenings. The trial of Lieut Stoughten will resume again at eight oclock tomorrow AM. Last night I had to get up in the night and put on my cloths to help keep me warm and had two thick woollen blankets over me and tonight is agoing to be the same. I have got coat and blows [blouse] on to go to bed.

There was another squad of Negroes came in to day and was examined and sent to Negro Reg[imen]t.

Monday

Aug 31st. Today being the last day of the month we will have general or grand review which will be composed of all the troops at this post which is our Reg[imen]t or the 14th Iowa the 32nd Iowa 31st Wis[consin] 4th Mo [Missouri] Cav[alry] a Negro Reg[imen]t part of the 16th WS [Wisconsin?] Reg[imen]t all on review at once a very nice Sight.

Sundown. We mustered for pay this eve. It is fair and beautiful this evening. I think that it will not be so cold tonight as usual. I would say that tomorrow is pay day but we dont expect our money for some days.

Tuesday

Sept 1st. All qu[i]et today at this place. It has been quite ↑warm ↓althoug very pleasant↑ today.↓ I took a general stroll today. Was walking pretty much all day got in at 4 pm. Had good dress perade which is just over and I have returned to my tent. It is now about sundown. The gun will fire in a few minutes. The trial of Lie[u]t[enant]

Stoughten is over but the decission or verdict is not rendered to the parties or public.[55] There was a Reg[imen]t passed down on board a transport this evening said to be the 3d Arkansas Inf[an]t[ry] Vol[unteer]s. This is the day that government proposes to pay but the money is not here yet. This evening is one of those that is Scarce ever found ecept in the Sunny south. A little Smoky looks like an evening in indian summer and it is pleasant and cool. Guard duty is not quite so heavy now as it was some time since.

Wednesday

Sept 2nd. It has been quite warm today uncomfortably so. It feels as though summer had returned in its rigor after our little Spell of cold weather and I think Judging from present apearances that we are agoing to have Some warm weather again which will be very unwelcome to the army at this place.

Thursday

Sept 3d. Quite warm today although very comfortable. I have Just been changing tents and have got my furniture fixed up. After some time working I have got split boards to lay on now in

55. Second Lieutenant William Stoughton resigned January 23, 1864, just before the regiment left Fort Halleck for Vicksburg, Tennessee.

place of poles that I have before Spoken of which I think will go some better. There was about 50 persons Gentlemen and ladies came here to day to visit fort hallack. They came on an excursion from northern Ill[inoi]s. They stopped inside the for[t] for some time and sung several very apropriate ballads which was very nice for which they received uprorous cheers from the Soldiery of this place. They went from the fort down town again. I dont know when they think of returning home as I was busy and did not convers with any of them. There was a Sergeant belonging to the 31st Wis[consin] Vol[unteer]s consigned to the tombs this evening. The funeral escort passed our Reg[imen]t when on dress perade a few minutes ago to the slow time of the dead march. There is three negroes to be hung tomorrow at this place for the slaughter of a family of whites at Island No 10 some months ago and I suppose that the Spirit of John Brown will be there ready to take them immediately after death and muster them into the army of the lord as he goes marching along and I wish them a happy voyage over the river of Jordan after we take from them their lives and their reath of glory they expected to wear around their neck and substitute for it a reath of hemp for that is all we can do as they have but one life. If they had more I would say take more from them.[56]

Friday

Sept 4th. This morning opened up very pleasant but I think that it will be quite warm today. 9 oclock AM. I Start for the execution of the three negroes I Spoke of yesterday.

I arrived there and they was just errecting the gallows. They got it ready and sent for the criminals which arrived in about an hour and by this time the crowd was de[n]se. I took my position about 30 rods from the gallows and finally thought that I would get close up to it and done so by crowding my way through and got to a wagon and asked leaf to stand on the wheel and they made room for me and Lieut[enant] Miles in the wagon and then we had good view at a short distance form [*sic*] the scene. Finally we heard the drum beatting the dead march and looked with anxious eyes until the procession came to the top of the ↑hill↓ so we could see in what way they

56. On Aug. 4, 1863, contraband soldiers living at a camp on Island No. 10 went to Compromise Landing and murdered six members of the Beckham family. Newspaper accounts say one or more white men instigated the attack. "Murder by Negro Soldiers; A FAMILY ASSASSINATED IN COLD BLOOD," *New York Times,* August 14, 1863; "Negro Soldiers," *The Age,* January 9, 1864.

brought the criminals. They was in a comon lumber wagon sitting on their coffins with their hands tied two guards in the wagon with them and a file of soldiers in front and a file in rear of the wagon. They looked very penetent and when they went on the scaffold accompanied by two Negro preachers they ↑looked↓ still more sorry than ever. The preachers sung and prayed ↑and↓ the provost martial proceeded to do his work fastening the rope upon their neck and the white sack over their head. Then he went down and moved the ladder. Now ↑he is↓ nerved up for he ↑has↓ takes [*sic*] out his knife to cut the cord that s[rest of word erased] Supports the scaffold. He cuts it. They take their last fall. You hear a dull sound caused by the tension of the ropes and one of them scarcely struggles atal. The other to strugles violently for a few moments. Then all is over and I got down and Started back to camp (leaving them hanging) to which place I arrived at two oclock layed down to [letter "a" covered with proofreader's deletion symbol] rest a couple hours and we had a good dress perade at the usual time half past five oclock. There was one man detailed out of our Co[mpany] this evening to attend a funeral escort. I dont know who diseased was. I presume he died at the post or general hospital.

Saturday

Sept 5th. Tolerable pleasant today though quite warm in the middle of the day but cool and pleasant this evening. I Rec[eive]d a letter this morning which contained a picture of my wife and youngest child[57] which I answered Sending a picture of myself in return also a little book to my daughter Clara. I went to the hospital this evening to see the Sick as I do frequently. I found them all on the mend ecept one Christopher Davidson a member of our Co[mpany]. I think he will not live many days.

Sunday

Sept 6th. All Still to day. Quite warm and very lonesom. We had good dress perade which is just over and the evening gun has fired.

Monday

Sept 7th. Last night our Co[mpany] lost the first man by death. Davidson that I Spoke of being Sick Some days ago died last night about midnight.[58] This morning was quite cool but

57. It is not known whether this picture still exists.

58. Christopher F. Davidson of Waterloo, Iowa, age 18, died of typhoid fever September 6, 1863. He was mustered into Company C when Spawr was.

warmer in the middle of the day. There is a great deal of ague in camp and Seems to be on the increase very fast. This after noon at 3 oclock the prcession Started with the remains of poor Davidson. We got to the grave yard (I Say we for I was along and all of the company that was not on duty or Sick went as mourners). We found a hole dug not long anough to let the coffin in and no vault. They cut it out at the end So as to let the coffin in fired three volleys over the grave and prceeded to fill it up which I did not Stop to see for it was getting along toward dress perade time but it was a very large grave yard.

Tuesday

Sept 8th. It has been very warm today. I think almost as warm as any day we have had Since we have been at this place. There has nothing of note occured today. I hear to day from official Source the expatation is that we will go to Cairo in a few days and probly Spend the winter there which news would be very thankfully rec[eive]d by the Reg[imen]t for there we will get good barracks which is much better than tents.

Wednesday

Sept 9th. This is another very warm day. However about noon a Strong gale came up from the north that cooled things of[f] Some but it is hot yet although the wind blows hard and the whole air is full of dust. There is a circus came to columbus to day and will Show tonight I understand and Some of the boys is gowing down to See it. One more of our co[mpany] got a furlough today and intends starting home tomorrow morning. His name is H W Beckwith 2nd Seargeant of our co[mpany].[59] Ague Still gets worse all the time. I believe [---] 11 men from our co[mpany] Sick.

Thursday

Sept 10th. The anouncement was made that we would move out of the fort which we done in due form. We moved about one mile and a half and camped on the ground or near the ground that the negroes was hung last friday and tomorrow I understand that there will be thre[e] more Swung on the gallows which is Standing as a warning to all men.

Friday

Sept 11th. It is very warm to day. We have been fixing up all day in our new camp. The three Negroes was not hung today for Some cause. We

59. Second Sergeant Henry Beckwith of Butler Center, Iowa, age 27. Mustered into Company C when Spawr was.

Still get a great many rumors about moving from Columbus. Some Say up and Some Say down the river.

Saturday

Sept 12th. 12 oclock M. Quite warm this forenoon although there is a cloud raising in the west and it is thundering very steady and I think that it will rain heavy and be cooler. A member of Co[mpany] A in our Reg[imen]t died last night in hospital.[60] Two men was buried to day. I think I will like our Camp very well. We are Situated in an orchard. There has been a good farm at this place but nothing is left to tell except apple trees and weeds and there is a good Spring about 1/4 of a mile from the camp.

Sunday

Sept 13th. Quite cool and pleasant today owing to a light Shower we had last night.

Monday

Sept 14th. All quiet today. Cool in the morning and warm in the middle of the day.

---

60. Eighth Corporal Leonard Lavender of Walcott, Iowa, died of dysentery September 11, 1863. His body was later moved to the National Cemetery, Mound City, Illinois, Section C, grave 3084.

Tuesday

Sept 15th. Quite cool this morning but very warm at noon.

[This is the last entry and the next to the last page in the book. At the bottom of this page, he had turned it upside down and written "Valentine L. Spawr." On the last page (upside down), he had written a list with the heading "Amts due me." The list contained last names and amounts. It appears only the first two were crossed off. The page is water stained and hard to read. There were 12 entries; most were for $40.[61]]

Then What Happened?

Soon after Spawr made the last entry in his diary, he requested a thirty-day furlough to travel to McLean County, Illinois. The request was for "the most serious illness of his family and meritorious conduct," his commanding officer wrote on the form he forwarded. The author assumes this trip was related to the child his wife feared would not survive, but she has not learned any more. Army records show he was granted the furlough on September 16; an added note says it was only for twenty days, not the thirty he requested.

---

61. About two months' pay.

Spawr's pension file shows he was detached and on duty at a soldiers' home in November and December, presumably the one in Columbus. The U.S. Sanitary Commission had established soldiers' homes to provide temporary housing and meals at no charge for traveling soldiers and former soldiers.[62]

62. Shambaugh, *Mississippi Valley Historical Association,* 223, 263.

PART 2
WHEN HEROIC VALOR IS REQUIRED

Levee and steamboats, Vicksburg, Mississippi, February 1864. Wm. R. Pywell, photographer (Library of Congress).

CHAPTER 1

THE MERIDIAN EXPEDITION: DOING AS MUCH DAMAGE AS POSSIBLE

Company C enlisted twenty-six local men at Fort Halleck in the last few months of 1863. As the end of the year approached, Kentucky was struggling to raise its quota of 12,000 men before the draft was ordered January 5, 1864, under the Enrollment Act. Kentucky Governor Thomas Bramlette proclaimed that those who volunteered to join an old regiment would receive a bounty of $300 but anyone who waited to be drafted would receive nothing. Seven of the new Company C recruits were mustered in January 4 or January 5; of those, five deserted within a few weeks.

Garrison duty at Fort Halleck finally ended for the Fourteenth Iowa on January 24, 1864, when the men boarded a steamer to travel down the Mississippi from Columbus, Kentucky, to Vicksburg, Mississippi. They made the trip in about six days and camped outside the breastworks on the east side of the city.[63]

The regiment was now part of the Third Division (commanded by Brigadier General Andrew Jackson Smith) of the Sixteenth Army Corps (commanded by Major General Stephen A. Hurlbut). The Fourteenth, Twenty-Seventh, and Thirty-Second Iowa and the Twenty-Fourth Missouri infantries formed the Second Brigade of the Third Division. Colonel William T. Shaw was moved up to command the brigade, which would become known to some during the coming battles as the "Iron Brigade." Lieutenant Colonel Joseph H. Newbold replaced Shaw as commander of the Fourteenth.[64]

Action at Last

The Fourteenth's replacement companies saw their first action—and the older companies saw their first action since the battles of Shiloh and Corinth—soon after arriving at Vicksburg. Major General William Tecumseh Sherman, commander of the Army of the Tennessee, used parts of the

---

63. Ingersoll, 200; "From the 32nd Iowa Regiment," signed "A. T.," *Waterloo (Iowa) Courier*, March 23, 1864.

64. Except where noted otherwise, the information for this chapter is from R. Scott, "Meridian, Miss., Expedition." Details about members of the regiment are from Thrift, *Roster and Record,* 731–879.

Sixteenth and Seventeenth Army Corps (commanded by Major General James B. McPherson) in his Meridian Raid across Mississippi. "My object was to break up the enemy's railroads at and about Meridian, and to do the enemy as much damage as possible in the month of February," Sherman wrote. Then he was to assist Major General Nathaniel Banks in the Department of the Gulf in doing the same in Red River country, especially Shreveport. The idea was to strengthen Union control along the Mississippi River and enable some of the troops along it to be used elsewhere.

The field orders Sherman issued for the Meridian expedition were clear.

> The command designated for the field will be lightly equipped—no tents or luggage save what is carried by the officers, men, and horses. Wagons must be reserved for food and ammunition. Cartridge boxes must be filled full of fresh ammunition and a hundred rounds extra carried along in wagons or on pack animals. Ten days' meat and bread and thirty days' . . . salt, sugar, and coffee will be carried in wagons; beef-cattle driven along.

Foraging was not mentioned, but it would be unavoidable. "The command was almost entirely subsisted on the country during the march," Hurlbut reported after they returned.

The Sixteenth Army Corps's Third Division—including the Fourteenth Iowa—and part of the Fourth Division joined part of the Seventeenth Army Corps heading east out of Vicksburg on February 3. Hurlbut's column crossed the Big Black River at Messinger's, and skirmishing began as soon as they were over the river. They entered Meridian the afternoon of February 14 after yet another skirmish just outside of town.[65]

"For five days 10,000 men worked hard and with a will in that work of destruction with axes, crowbars, sledges, clawbars, and with fire," Sherman reported. The men of the Sixteenth worked north and east of town while the troops of the Seventeenth did the same to the south and west. The Sixteenth destroyed sixty miles of railroad as far as fifteen miles east to Cuba Station and twenty miles north to Lauderdale Springs as well as destroying a locomotive and burning eight bridges. "All hands [were] engaged in destroying rebel property, tearing up and bending railroad iron, and foraging for the army," a member of the Thirty-Second Iowa signing the

65. "From the 32nd Iowa Regiment."

initials "A. T." wrote to the *Waterloo (Iowa) Courier*.[66]

A *Chicago Tribune* correspondent described the destruction of the railroad in more detail.[67] Meridian's importance, he wrote, was the result of the Mobile and Ohio Railroads intersecting the Southern Railroad there. They were a means of communication and a supply route for the Confederates. Sherman's men tore up the iron rails and then dug up the wooden ties that had been beneath them. They piled them together with the ties on the ground and the rails laid across them and set fire to them. As the rails got hot, they softened and the ends sank. They could not be used after they cooled in that shape, and the Confederates had little iron to make new replacements. The Union soldiers destroyed at least a dozen miles of railroad this way in each direction from the town as well as at other locations on their way there and back.

They began the march back to Vicksburg on February 20, encountering dusty roads on some days and cold rain and sloppy mud on another day. They discovered there was little to forage

66. Dated March 6, 1864; published March 23.

67. "The Great Mississippi Expedition. Full Particulars from Our Correspondent. The Occupation of Jackson, Brandon, Meridian and Camden. The Results of the Expedition—Destruction of Property and Loss of Life," March 14, 1864.

because the advance had stripped the surrounding country. They arrived back at Vicksburg on March 4.[68]

The letter from "A. T." summarized what they had done.

> The expedition accomplished all, and more than was expected of it. Over a hundred miles of railroad was effectually destroyed and as much more of telegraph. Fifteen locomotives and thirty or forty cars were demolished; and a dozen depots, water tanks, etc., were destroyed. At Meridan [*sic*] a large number of Government warehouses and other public buildings were burned. Upwards of 200 cotton gin houses were destroyed and almost any amount of cotton. The towns of Hillsborough and Decatur were almost entirely burned down, and the business part of New Meridan [*sic*] suffered the same fate. Besides this there were many buildings burned without any authority for it, so that to say the least, the Southern Confederacy is not so wealthy by at least $200,000,000 as they were before the expedition passed through. Mississippi is effectually wrested from the rebellion so far as

68. Albert Underwood Civil War Diary, transcribed by Mr. Ralph Williams, http://www.artilleryreserve.org/main/Underwood.pdf.

furnishing any supplies to the rebel army is concerned.

"Meridian with its depots, store houses, arsenal, hospitals, offices, hotels, and cantonments no longer exists," Sherman reported. His summary of the accomplishments of the expedition is similar to the *Courier* letter writer's.

> We beat the enemy wherever he opposed or offered resistance. We drove him out of Mississippi, destroyed the only remaining railroads in the State, the only roads by which he could maintain an army in Mississippi threatening to our forces or the main river. We subsisted our army and animals chiefly on his stores, brought away about 400 prisoners and full 5,000 negroes, about 1,000 white refugees, about 3,000 animals (horses, mules, and oxen), and any quantity of wagons and vehicles. . . .
>
> The great result attained is the hardihood and confidence imparted to the command, which is now better fitted for war. Animals and men returned to Vicksburg after marching from 360 to 450 miles in the space of the shortest month in the year, in better health and condition than when we started.

Although Sherman described the expedition as "more of the character of a pleasant excursion than of hard military service," the Sixteenth Corps had five men killed, twenty-one wounded, and twenty-six missing. None of the killed or wounded were in the Fourteenth Iowa, but nineteen of its members were among the missing. Many of the missing were in Company C. Asahel McAllister was taken prisoner February 10, and John Bartal, Cornelius Boylan, and Fred Buckmaster were captured February 17. Bartal was an 18-year-old Cairo, Illinois, man who had just enlisted December 1, 1863. McAllister and Boylan ended up in the new Confederate prison at Andersonville, Georgia, where McAllister died June 16, 1864, and Boylan died September 21, 1864; both were buried there. Bartal and Buckmaster returned to service. John C. Miller of Davenport was listed as "missing and taken prisoner" March 1; the Army had no further record.

Nine of the Columbus recruits deserted during the expedition. Andrew Fisk, a 19-year-old Columbus man who had enlisted December 3, 1863, died of chronic diarrhea in Decatur, Mississippi, on February 23.

The Meridian expedition was the first time Sherman chose to march without a supply line and to destroy everything within a swath of Confederate territory. He would use the same methods in his notorious March to the Sea in Georgia at the end of that year.

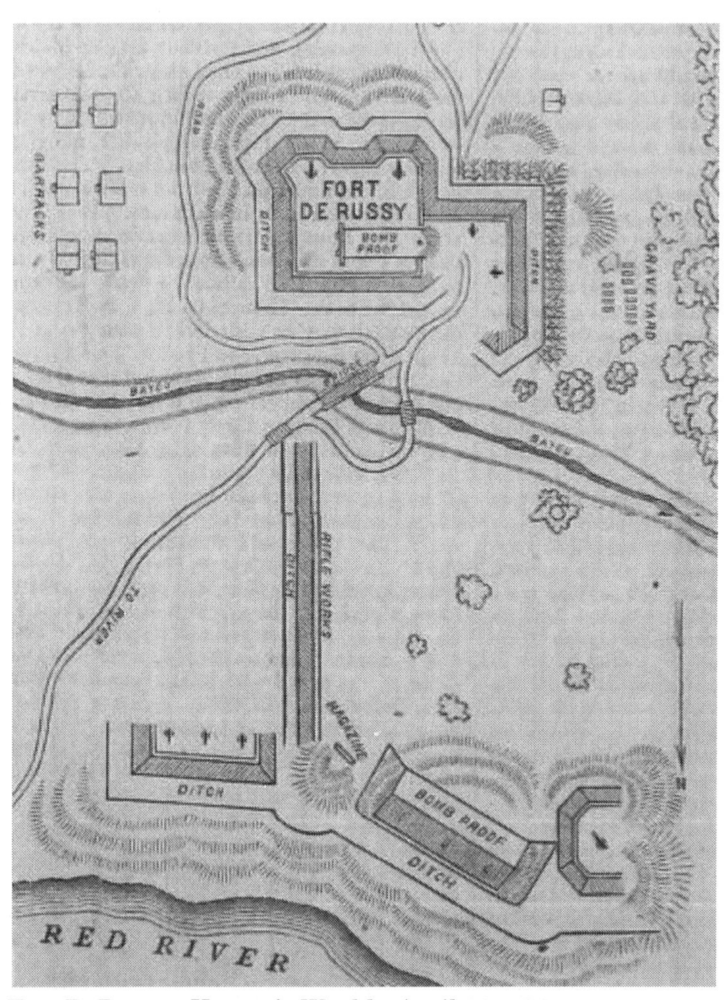

Fort DeRussy, *Harper's Weekly,* April 30, 1864.

CHAPTER 2

FORT DERUSSY:
FORWARD, DOUBLE-QUICK, MARCH!

The troops at Vicksburg were "preparing for another grand expedition" March 10, said a report in the Davenport, Iowa, *Daily Democrat and News*.[69] "The troops are in excellent spirits, and eager for marching orders."

Major General Nathaniel Banks, commander of the Army of the Gulf, was ready to launch the Red River Campaign (also known as the Red River Expedition). The goals of Banks's campaign included capturing Shreveport, Louisiana, from the Confederates; controlling the Red River; being in a position to occupy Texas; and confiscating cotton from plantations. He needed some troops from Major General William T. Sherman's Army of the Tennessee, so Sherman sent a detachment under the command of Brigadier General A. J. Smith. It comprised about 10,000 troops from the Second and Third Brigades of the First Division of the Sixteenth Corps, the Third Division of the

69. "Late News," March 17, 1864.

Sixteenth Corps, an artillery made up of a couple of Indiana batteries, and a provisional division of the Seventeenth Army Corps that contained two brigades and a battery. Brigadier General Joseph A. Mower was moved up to command both the Third Division (of which the Fourteenth Iowa was a part) and the partial First Division of the Sixteenth.[70]

Red River

The Red River runs through Louisiana from the northwest to the southeast. Shreveport, which is on the Red River, is about 175 miles due east of Vicksburg, which is on the Mississippi River. But rather than marching cross-country to Shreveport, the Union troops traveled south on the Mississippi to the mouth of the Red River. They embarked on transports on Wednesday, March 9, and started steaming down the Mississippi the next day. The Fourteenth Iowa was on the *William L. Ewing*, No. 10 in a fleet of twenty steamers. The Second Brigade left Vicksburg at about 6 p.m. Thursday, March 10, and arrived at the mouth of the Red River about

70. Byers, *Iowa in War Times,* 174–175; R. Scott, "Meridian, Miss., Expedition," 190; unless otherwise noted, the information in this chapter is from R. Scott, "Operations in Louisiana and Trans-Mississippi," 162–638.

noon the following day. Twenty gunboats—a portion of the Mississippi Squadron—were there ahead of them.[71]

The original plan was for Smith to travel up the Red River to Alexandria. When he and Admiral David Porter met, however, he learned that Fort DeRussy, a fort on the river halfway between there and Alexandria, had been garrisoned by the Confederates and needed to be taken before they could proceed. "It was therefore deemed best," Smith wrote in his report without specifying who deemed it so, "to act against it in conjunction, the army in the rear by land and the navy by river."

The next day, Saturday, March 12, the troops entered the mouth of Red River at about noon and traveled up it until they reached a segment of Red River then called "Old River." They turned south on that and followed it, convoyed by nine of the gunboats, to the mouth of the Atchafalaya River. Traveling south on the Atchafalaya, they saw plantations on the banks of the river, "some of them exhibiting evidence of taste quite unlooked

---

71. "From the Red River Expedition. Capture of Fort DeRussy—The Rebel Prospects in Louisiana Gloomy," correspondence of the *St. Louis Republican,* in *Nashville Daily Union,* April 2, 1864; "Red River Expedition," from a private letter dated March 23, 1864, and signed "Frank" in *Centralia (Illinois) Sentinel,* April 14, 1864.

for," a *Chicago Tribune* correspondent wrote.[72] "A few white women were to be seen, the men were absent." About twelve miles down the river they reached the remnants of Simmesport, a town on the right bank near the mouth of Bayou des Glaises and twenty-five miles by land from Fort DeRussy. They landed there at about 5 p.m. that day. Other than a few chimneys marking the site, the town itself did not actually exist anymore. The previous year it had been burned by Colonel Charles Rivers Ellet because his boat had been fired on from there. His cousin, Colonel John Ellet, during the siege of Port Hudson, had finished destroying it.

When they had arrived at the mouth of the Red River the previous evening, the troops had rounded up all the animals they would be able to butcher, and then they had set fire to the houses. After arriving at Simmesport, they "tied up again and again went out foraging," Samuel H. Thomas of the Twenty-Seventh Iowa wrote to his family.[73] "I should not be a faithful historian if I omitted to mention that the conduct of the troops, since the late raid of Gen. Sherman, is becoming very

72. "From Gen. Banks' Department. The Expedition to West Louisiana: A Formidable Fleet of Gunboats—Operations on the Atchafalaya—Further Details from Fort DeRussy," April 1, 1864.

73 Thomas, "A First-Hand Account of the Capture of Fort DeRussy," http://www.fortderussy.org/thomas_letter.html.

prejudicial to our good name and their efficiency," an anonymous correspondent for the *St. Louis Republican* commented.[74]

> A spirit of destruction and wanton ferocity seems to have seized upon many of them, which is quite incredible. At Red River Landing they robbed a house of several thousand dollars in specie, and then fired the house to conceal their crime. At Simmsport [*sic*], a party of them stole out and robbed and insulted a family two miles distant. . . . I am glad to say that General Smith is disposed to punish all offenders severely.

The next day, Sunday, March 13, Smith sent out the divisions of the Sixteenth Corps, including the Fourteenth Iowa, under Brigadier General Joseph A. Mower to look for the Confederates and see the condition of the route. They passed a couple of deserted rebel camps, and several miles from the landing they came upon a fort under construction at the fork of the Bayou des Glaises and the Yellow Bayou (called Fort Morgan in Thomas's letter). The Confederate brigade working on it fled at Mower's approach, leaving a bridge over the bayou burning. The Union troops

74. "From the Red River Expedition. Capture of Fort DeRussy—The Rebel Prospects in Louisiana Gloomy."

chased them a couple of miles and overtook five wagons loaded with tents. They burned the tents and loaded up the wagons with sugar and molasses, which the rebels had tried to destroy, according to the *St. Louis Republican.* They also took about twenty prisoners before returning to the boats.

March to Fort DeRussy

At dark the troops received orders to be ready to march that evening. A soldier from the Forty-Ninth Illinois, in a private letter signed only "Frank" in the *Centralia (Illinois) Sentinel,* wrote that they "drew rations to include the 28th, but took nothing with [them] but hard bread, seventy-five rations of bacon, salt and coffee." These rations must have been for the whole regiment, because this soldier added that all he took was a horse blanket and overcoat. Thomas wrote that after supper they got their blankets and forty rounds of cartridges. "You must know that 5 miles with our load is as hard as 15 miles without," he complained in his letter. The troops left Simmesport at about 9 p.m., marched about four miles, and bivouacked for the night. At the same time, Smith directed the transports to return to Red River and join the Mississippi Squadron to proceed with it up the river to Fort

DeRussy. The troops did not learn their destination until they were marching the next day.

Early the next morning, Monday, March 14, Colonel William T. Shaw's Second Brigade, including the Fourteenth Iowa, was ordered to "take the advance in line of march" toward Fort DeRussy, which was still about twenty miles away.[75] They headed out at 6 a.m., moving northwest overland in light marching order.

The Bayou des Glaises lay next to the road for a time and then turned to the north. The troops traveled "through beautiful country, abounding in large sugar plantations, with their sugar houses, etc.," the soldier in the Forty-Ninth Illinois wrote. He continued, "No straggling is permitted, men march rapidly, there are but few halts, ranks are well closed." The Confederate forces fell back as Shaw's brigade advanced. A couple of times the advance troops came to bridges the rebels had set on fire to delay them, but they were able to extinguish them before much damage was done.

As the Union soldiers approached the town of Mansura, the road intersected with Bayou des Glaises again with the bayou now crossing the

75. Reports written at the time appear to exaggerate the distance, claiming the march was up to thirty-five miles. Modern maps show the distance between Simmesport and Fort DeRussy to be twenty-five miles.

road. A rebel division of about six or eight hundred men commanded by Major General John Walker had marched there from the fort. The Confederates had burned the bridge across the bayou and were waiting on the opposite bank where they thought Smith's force would try to cross. Shaw ordered forward the Third Indiana Battery with a regiment of infantry, and they opened fire on the rebels. That cleared the bank, and Shaw was able to cross the infantry using a scow they had left undamaged. At the same time, he had the pioneer corps build a new bridge for the artillery and teams using materials from an old cotton gin. The column was across the bayou within two hours. As soon as the artillery had crossed, Shaw pushed on.

More than one participant in this march commented on the beautiful scenery. General T. Kilby Smith, commanding the division of the Seventeenth and bringing up the rear of the column, described it in his report.

> Now crossing the bayou and penetrating a swamp for a few miles, we suddenly emerged on one of the most beautiful prairies imaginable, high table land, gently undulating, watered by little lakes, with occasional groves, the landscape dotted with tasteful houses, gardens and shrubberies. This prairie,

called Avoyelles, is settled exclusively by French emigrants, many of whom, as our army passed, sought shelter under the tricolor of France.

It was not until then that the troops learned their destination was Fort DeRussy, according to letter writer "Frank" of the Forty-Ninth Illinois.

Attack

The Fourteenth Iowa, "on the advance" as part of the Second Brigade, marched the last two miles "on the double quick." At about 4 p.m. they came within range of the guns of the fort and halted briefly. Shaw had the Third Indiana Battery take up position on the road and start firing. Smith directed Mower to advance with the First and Second Brigades (including Shaw's) of the Third Division in line of battle. For support, Companies D and I of the Fourteenth Iowa were ordered to deploy as skirmishers over the wet, swampy ground to the right of the road. Shaw positioned the other regiments of his brigade, the Twenty-Seventh Iowa and the Twenty-Fourth Missouri, to the left of the Fourteenth. The Third Brigade of the Third Division followed within supporting distance.[76]

When the skirmishers reached the outer works, within 350 yards of the main fort, the rebels opened fire on them from the fort with five pieces of artillery. Lieutenant Colonel Joseph H. Newbold, commander of the Fourteenth, sent out Company K to the left of his first skirmishers, where they had to take up position in a swamp. A company of the Thirty-Second Iowa joined them. The skirmishers "took possession of a line of rifle pits about two hundred yards from the main fort which movement enabled me to greatly annoy the enemy's gunners. At this time the fire was exceedingly brisk from both artillery and musketry but it was replied to with equal energy and rapidity from the fort," Shaw wrote in his report. But "their guns on the land side all being en barbette [behind a low wall], the skirmishers of the Second Brigade soon silenced them," Smith reported.

"In line of battle, a quarter of a mile from the inner works of the rebels, our regiment and the Thirty-Second Iowa advanced to near the ditches or outer works, when the rebel batteries and musketry opened heavy fire upon us," First

---

76. Lieutenant Orville Burke, Company H, Fourteenth Iowa, "From the 14th Regiment," letter to the editor dated March 16, 1864, *Anamosa (Iowa) Eureka,* April 8, 1864.

Lieutenant Orville Burke of Company H, Fourteenth Iowa, wrote in a letter to the editor of the *Anamosa (Iowa) Eureka* ("From the 14th Regiment," April 8, 1864). The firing went on for a couple of hours.

Newbold moved the Fourteenth forward when the firing became heavy on the extreme left of the line. The Twenty-Seventh Iowa, which had stayed behind in Marksville long enough to act as guards until the army had passed through, had arrived and joined the battle. "The din was terrific," Thomas wrote. "The Rebel shot and shell came crashing through the Belt of woods which surrounded the fort throwing The dirt in our eyes 'right smart' and no mistake. We were ordered to fall on our faces which we did."

Victory

Finally, Mower sent his brigades that had been in the rear around to the other side of the fort to cut off escape there. He commanded the First and Second Brigades to fix bayonets and advance in the line of battle at a double-quick. As soon as they reached the edge of the timber in front of the west side of the fort, they were ordered to "charge bayonets" across the open field in front of them. "In our way was an open space of 100 yds and all along were felled trees. We started and amid a shower of balls from the musketry gained the ditch surrounding the fort," Thomas wrote.

"It was a long way to the fort," Colonel James I. Gilbert of the Twenty-Seventh wrote in his report.

> The ground over which we must charge was well cleared of trees. Many logs lay on the ground, and several ditches were to be crossed. At the command, "Forward, double-quick, march!" the entire regiment sprang forward with a will. . . . We sprang into the ditch on the east and south sides of the fort, and mounted the parapet in all haste.

There was scattered fire from the rebels, but the skirmishers kept it down. The men crossed the ditch around the fort and clambered over the parapet into it. "The ditch was 10 feet deep the sides perpendicular and the wall of the fort rising 25 ft high," according to Thomas. "The men sprang into the ditch and by picking and scratching a few got partly up then grasped the guns of their companions and soon the walls were black with men." (The wall was 20 feet high, according to Major John C. Becht, commander of the Fifth Minnesota infantry.) The final charge took less than twenty minutes.

The regiments vied with each other to be the first in the fort, and different reports of the battle name different regiments as accomplishing it. According to Mower, regiments of First Brigade, Third Division, beat the Twenty-Fourth Missouri of Shaw's Second Brigade by half a minute. The latter had been momentarily delayed by an abatis—an obstacle made by felled trees with pointed branches facing in their direction. "There was not, however, a difference of half a minute in the time of planting the colors by the different regiments," Mower reported later. He said a bayou prevented the Fourteenth Iowa and the rest of the troops that had moved up on the right of the road from getting into the works as soon as the others.

"I know of my own personal knowledge that Fort De Russy was captured by Col. Shaw's brigade and the 14th, 27th and 32d Iowa were the first to mount its walls," T. C. McCall, quartermaster of the Thirty-Second Iowa, wrote in a letter to the *Iowa State Register* May 14, 1864.[77]

The Fourteenth's Burke described the scene.

> In less than five minutes the colors of the Twenty-Fourth Missouri were hoisted on the

77. Quoted in Shaw, "Battle of Pleasant Hill," 423.

> parapets. The 14th boys came into the Fort next, whooping and yelling, jumping over logs, brush and rifle pits as fast as they could. Up the sides of the embankments they advanced; and, with a general war whoop from all sides, in the brave boys of the Union came, regiment after regiment, and compelled the rebs to surrender.

"When the fort was surrendered a part of my regiment, with others of other regiments, joined in a fire of musketry, and with them united in a wild, ringing, vociferous yell of joy," Gilbert wrote.

"Now and not till now did the Rebels cease fighting and show the white flag another moment and not one would have lived to tell the story," Thomas boasted.

At the same time, the boats that had been traveling up the river to meet them arrived, too late to help. They had been delayed by obstructions placed in the river.

Gains and Losses

Smith listed what they accomplished: "We captured 319 prisoners, 10 pieces of artillery, and a large quantity of ordnance and ordnance stores, marching during the day 26 miles, bridging a bayou, and capturing the fort before sunset."

The replacement companies of the Fourteenth had been through their first battle. No one in the Fourteenth Iowa was killed in the action; in fact, only three of Smith's soldiers were killed that day. Thirty-five were wounded; of those, Peter D. Shmidt of Hickory Grove, Iowa, a private in Company A, was injured in the right shoulder and died of his wounds in Memphis on May 13.[78]

The troops of the Sixteenth Corps got back on the transports the evening of the next day, March 15, to head up the river to Alexandria. When they arrived the day after that, they found the city had been evacuated just a few hours earlier. They stayed on their boats while they waited for Smith, who had remained at the fort with the Seventeenth Corps to dismantle it. He reached Alexandria at about 5 p.m. on March 18 and had the troops disembark and set up camp. There they waited for Banks.

"Frank" of the Forty-Ninth Illinois wrote to his friend March 23. "Our boys are foraging extensively," he said. The regiment "is just returning from two long and tedious campaigns," he concluded. "It has passed without tents or shelter of any kind, and part of the time on very scant rations."

---

78. Thrift, *Roster and Record,* 755–781.

When Banks arrived on March 26, he had Smith march his command to Cotile Landing, Louisiana. They left on the Bayou Rapids road on March 28 with rations for three days and marched eighteen miles. The next day they marched nine miles and reached the landing. They camped there until transports arrived on April 2 (the sixth day on three days' rations), and they headed up the river to Grand Ecore, arriving the next day, and camped above the town until April 7.[79] They started to march to Shreveport that day, but Confederate Major General Richard "Dick" Taylor would make sure they never made it.

79. John Scott, Appendix E in *Report of Adjutant General, 1865–1866,* 307.

Attack on General Albert L. Lee's wagon train near Mansfield, Louisiana, April 8, 1864. C. E. H. Bonwill, *Frank Leslie's Illustrated Newspaper,* New York, May 21, 1864 (Library of Congress).

CHAPTER 3
MANSFIELD, LOUISIANA: FIGHTING A LARGE BATTLE WITH WAGON TRAINS

Leaving the provisional division of the Seventeenth Corps with the boats on the Red River, Brigadier General A. J. Smith began the march to Shreveport Thursday, April 7, with his two divisions of the Sixteenth Corps. Major General Nathaniel Banks, commander of the Army of the Gulf, had his troops start out the day before: three cavalry brigades commanded by Brigadier General Albert L. Lee, two small divisions of the Thirteenth Corps under Brigadier General Thomas E. G. Ransom, and the First Division of the Nineteenth Corps under Brigadier General William H. Emory (marching in that order).

The First Division of the First Brigade of the Corps d'Afrique, often referred to as the "colored brigade," was also on the march and probably at the rear that day. The men of the brigade were used to build roads and bridges, but they were armed and trained to fight as well.

How many men fought for each side at Mansfield (and at Pleasant Hill the next day)? It depends on the person providing the number. Official reports, newspaper articles, old soldiers, and historians have never agreed. For example, the New Orleans *Daily True Delta*[80] estimated Confederate Major General Richard "Dick" Taylor had 18,000–22,000 men and Banks less than 6,000. Compare the newspaper's numbers with the ones recorded in the official records. Taylor, who commanded the District of West Louisiana in the Trans-Mississippi Theater, estimated he had 12,000 men when the 5,000 new troops arrived the evening of April 8 (after the battle of Mansfield but before the battle of Pleasant Hill). Banks, however, estimated in his report that at the battle at Mansfield—before the reinforcements had reached him—Taylor had 15,000 men. Based on an abstract from returns and rosters, Banks had more than 28,000 troops on the road with him: 5,333 in the cavalry, 5,265 in the Thirteenth, 7,414 in the Nineteenth, 1,745 in the Corps d'Afrique, and 8,582 in the Sixteenth. Without the Sixteenth at Mansfield on the first day, he had about 20,000 men.[81]

80. "The Great Battle in De Soto Parish," April 16, 1864.

81. Unless otherwise noted, the information in this chapter is from R. Scott, "Operations in Louisiana and Trans-Mississippi," 162–638.

When Smith's detachment overtook the column on April 7, it brought up the rear. Progress was slow and miserable because a heavy rain and the long wagon trains of supplies ahead of them had turned the roads into mud. But "everything progressed satisfactorily until about 2 o'clock P. M., when [they] encountered the head-quarters train of Major General Banks, entirely blocking the way, and hindering [their] progress," Colonel John Scott, commanding the Thirty-Second Iowa in Shaw's brigade, wrote.[82]

> The wagons were overloaded, and were said to contain articles ranging in weight from paper collars to iron bedsteads.
>
> In this manner two brigades, including artillery and trains, were delayed more than four hours, in the midst of heavy rain-storms. Finally the troops passed by in an effort to reach the assigned camping-ground before dark, but failed and camped two miles short of the proper position; subsistence and camp equipage did not come up until the night was far advanced.

---

82. John Scott, Appendix E in *Report of Adjutant General, 1865–1866,* 308.

The Sixteenth Corps had been able to travel only about eight miles that day.

"The idea of fighting a large battle with wagon trains, I don't think ever originated with any other man," correspondent "J. B. A." complained about Banks to the *Wisconsin State Journal* afterward.[83] Banks did not keep the detachments and trains closed up, so they stretched out for more than thirty miles. In other words, the last regiment was two days' travel behind the first.[84]

Trapped

Leaving at daylight the next morning, Friday, April 8, the Sixteenth continued west and marched twenty-one miles. A wagon train "long enough for transporting the troops of a good-sized army" delayed them for five hours, according to "J. E. H.," a correspondent of the *New York Tribune*.[85]

> It was only through the greatest personal exertions of Gen. Smith that his troops were hurried through the thick pine country, while

---

83. "From the Mississippi Squadron: The Red River Dam: Description of Its Construction and Passage—Evacuation and Burning of Atlanta—Passage down Red River," May 31, 1864.
84. Benson, "The Battle of Pleasant Hill, Louisiana," 483.
85. "The Battles in Louisiana," April 27, 1864.

> the narrow road was completely backed up with this long train, half of the wagons filled with trunks, chairs, valises, and other cumbersome baggage, such as greatly embarrass and oftentimes, as in the disaster of yesterday, imperil the lives of thousands of men.
>
> Finding the officers in charge were not competent men, Gen. Smith at once ordered Col. Shaw, commanding 3d Brigade [*sic*], to place the 14th Iowa Infantry in front with fixed bayonets, and, if necessary, fight their way through the road. Finding it useless to dally longer, the sleepy indigent crowd got waked up, and rather than submit to a bayonet charge, they concluded to "get up and git," as the soldiers say.

Smith did not describe this method of dealing with the traffic jam in his report.

It wasn't just the wagons of the Thirteenth and Nineteenth Corps blocking the road. Lee's train was ahead of them. Lee had repeatedly asked Major General William B. Franklin, the commanding officer of Banks's army, for permission to leave the cavalry train—about two hundred wagons—with the infantry following him, but Franklin never granted it. In fact, Franklin had directed Lee to proceed as far as possible that night—with his whole train—to give the infantry room to advance the next day. (In his report afterward, Banks blamed "the disasters of the day" on the "fatally incautious" presence of the cavalry train; neither he nor Franklin took responsibility for it.)

Smith and his men heard cannonading ahead of them late in the afternoon. Until then, the Confederates had been skirmishing with Banks's cavalry without letting him know there was a large force waiting for him. Taylor's plan succeeded: The skirmishers' running fire, Banks reported, never "develop[ed] the full strength of the enemy's forces or position." Several miles short of Mansfield, at Sabine Crossroads, a large rebel force surprised the cavalry and the Thirteenth Corps. Now "it became manifest that the enemy in full force and in strong position was in our front," Banks wrote later. When Smith heard the battle he sent word ahead to Franklin offering to bypass the train that was blocking him at the time so he could help. Franklin sent Emory's First Division of the Nineteenth instead.

The cavalry and the Thirteenth had to retreat, but about a mile from the battlefield they were blocked by a portion of the cavalry train stuck in the ruts and mud of the narrow road. Besides seizing 146 wagons and about 800 mules, the rebels took many prisoners including ambulances full of the wounded. The Union had already lost artillery during the fighting and lost the remaining guns that were trapped with the wagon train.

The Nineteenth fought the rebels until sunset. Banks implied his troops were the victors, saying the Nineteenth formed "an immovable wall of fire" on the crest of a hill and the Confederates retreated. And Franklin's report says Emory remained "master of the position" at the end of the day. Emory himself wrote in his report later that his division drove the rebels back and repulsed an effort to turn the left flank. Taylor's report, however, says the last thing his troops did was drive the Nineteenth off a ridge overlooking a creek and then four hundred yards farther. The rebels camped on the creek that night. Both sides needed the water.

Wild Night near Pleasant Hill

In the meantime, Smith received word that Banks was ordering the troops involved in the battle to withdraw to Pleasant Hill. Banks expected the fighting at Sabine Crossroads to resume early in the morning, and he was afraid Smith wouldn't be able to march his men the remaining fourteen miles in time to reach them before the army at the front was annihilated. The lack of water at Sabine Crossroads was another factor in Banks's decision.

Smith had his men "bivouac upon their arms" about two miles before reaching the town of Pleasant Hill and ordered them to be ready to march before daylight. The *New York Tribune* correspondent described their arrival.

> At sunset Friday [April 8] the sound of fifes and drums innumerable, whistling and beating their lively martial music, told of the arrival of "Whitey Smith," as the boys call him, and "Smith's Guerrillas," as they delight to be called. In an hour's time the troops were snugly encamped on the old Methodist camp meeting grounds, not, however, before a vigorous assault was made on the buildings, which disappeared as if by magic. There is a peculiar style of legerdemain practiced by our soldiers in relation to the procurement of firewood which must be seen to be appreciated.

The sounds of battle heard by the soldiers in the afternoon were not explained until hours later. "About 10 o'clock that night, we learned that the 13th Army Corps and Gen. Lee's cavalry had been attacked, badly cut up and driven back by the enemy, they being some twelve miles in advance of us," Thirty-Second Iowa quartermaster T. C. McCall wrote in a letter to the *Iowa State Register.*[86] "By one o'clock on the morning of the 9th a portion of Lee's cavalry and the train and the stragglers of the 13th Corps commenced passing our camp to the rear, and continued to do so until after daylight."[87]

"During the night our camp was overrun with stragglers from the front," Scott reported, "who circulated the wildest stories of disaster and loss of men, artillery and train. On the morning of the 9th these were repeated and exaggerated. The road was seen to be filled with teams crowding to the rear."

"Men, some hatless, ran, throwing away their guns and knapsacks as they ran, teamsters on mules, with harness dangling—all scared nearly out of their wits," Major Hugo Hoffbauer of the Fourteenth Iowa's Company A remembered.[88]

All but Brigadier General William Dwight's brigade left the battlefield at Sabine Crossroads by midnight; Emory had charged that brigade with forming the rear guard of the retreat. They

---

86. Written April 16, 1864, and published May 14.
87. "An Army Letter by Quartermaster T. C. McCall" in Shaw, "The Battle of Pleasant Hill," 419.
88. "Some Recollections of Red River Expedition, 1864," *Davenport (Iowa) Democrat and Leader,* April 9, 1915.

arrived back at Pleasant Hill about 8:30 Saturday morning.

Cheerless Morning

Banks sent the survivors in the Thirteenth, the Third and Fourth brigades of Lee's cavalry, several batteries, and possibly part of the Corps d'Afrique back to Grand Ecore with the wagon trains that morning. The *New York Tribune* said the reason Banks sent them away was the lack of subsistence for the troops and forage for the horses. Smith's divisions, part of the Nineteenth Corps, and at least part of the Corps d'Afrique remained. Banks ordered Smith's train to fall in with the rest of the wagons, but Smith refused to have a single team moved.[89]

The *New York Tribune* correspondent described the atmosphere.

> The weather on Saturday was most unpropitious for a fair fight. The morning air was intensely cold, and a more cheerless, disheartened sea of bronzed countenances I never beheld. Each private seemed to comprehend the vast magnitude of our needless disaster. There was a gloomy silence apparently pervading every camp, and we

89. McCall in Shaw, "The Battle of Pleasant Hill," 419.

could hear no gladsome shouts of victory ring through the decimated ranks. It is useless to deny that the universal opinion of the rank and file was that our repulse was an ignominious defeat, which ordinary generals might have foreseen and prevented.

The wind howled piteously through the trees, fanning the long pendants of gray, funereal-like moss which decked the tops of the tall, waving cypress and pines. The sky was shrouded with portentous clouds, while dense volumes of dust partially concealed the long pontoon trains as they rumbled heavily to the rear.

Battle of Pleasant Hill, Louisiana, *Harper's Weekly,* May 7, 1864.

CHAPTER 4

PLEASANT HILL: GENERAL, YOU HAVE SAVED THE ARMY

Pleasant Hill wasn't actually a hill; it was a plain about a mile square surrounded by woodland. Maps show a cluster of homes and other buildings along the road coming in from Grand Ecore to the east. The battlefield, west of the town, contained the plain and was about two miles across (east to west) and more than a mile north to south. The road leaving the town to the west, called the Mansfield (or Shreveport) Road, crossed the center of the battlefield. The modern town of Pleasant Hill lies about two and a half miles south of where the battle was fought.[90]

The New Orleans *Daily True Delta* described the battlefield as "a large, open field, which had

---

90. Unless otherwise noted, the sources for this chapter are letters and reports from R. Scott, "Operations in Louisiana and Trans-Mississippi," 162–638; letters and reports from Appendix E, *Report of Adjutant General, 1865–1866;* Shaw, "The Battle of Pleasant Hill"; and Benson, "The Battle of Pleasant Hill, Louisiana." Additional source for this paragraph: "The Battles in Louisiana," *New York Tribune,* April 27, 1864.

once been cultivated, but is now overgrown with weeds and bushes. The slightly elevated center of the field, from which the name Pleasant Hill is taken, is nothing more than a long mound, hardly worthy the name of a hill. A semi-circular belt of timber runs around the field on the Shreveport side." Colonel William T. Shaw described it as an old field, somewhat cut up with gullies and dotted with small pines. He said the woods on the opposite side consisted of "large timber, but rather scattering."

Brigadier General A. J. Smith, commander of the Sixteenth Army of the Tennessee detachment, marched the men of the Sixteenth the rest of the way from the Methodist campground to Pleasant Hill the morning of Saturday, April 9. About a half mile past the town, he joined General William H. Emory, commander of the three brigades of the Nineteenth Corps First Division, in forming a line of battle across the Mansfield Road. Emory placed his Third Brigade, commanded by Colonel Lewis Benedict, on the left. Brigadier General Joseph A. Mower, commanding the divisions of the Sixteenth, placed Colonel William F. Lynch's First Brigade, Third Division, of the Sixteenth Corps at Benedict's left flank and rear. The rest of his men were in reserve behind the line of battle along with several batteries.

Few of the reports mention it, but a company of soldiers of the Corps d'Afrique was deployed for skirmishing on the left before the battle.

Brigadier General William H. Emory, commander of the First Division of the Nineteenth Army Corps, had his other two brigades on the right—Brigadier General William Dwight's and Brigadier General James W. McMillan's. Major General Nathaniel P. Banks ordered Shaw to report to Emory with the Second Brigade, Third Division of the Sixteenth, and he did so at about 10 a.m. Shaw's brigade relieved McMillan's, which had been posted on the left of the Mansfield road and at right angles to it in a dense thicket. McMillan's brigade moved to the rear, nearly to the houses, to be in reserve. Dwight, commander of the First Brigade, First Division of the Nineteenth, had been posted on McMillan's right along a ravine diagonally to the rear. Emory had placed four guns of the Twenty-Fifth New York Battery about fifty yards to McMillan's front and on his right, on the left side of a ridge. They stayed. Shaw placed his regiments in the following order: the Twenty-Fourth Missouri under the command of Major Robert W. Fyan on the right, Fourteenth Iowa under Lieutenant Colonel Joseph H. Newbold at right center, Twenty-Seventh Iowa under Colonel

James I. Gilbert at left center, and Thirty-Second Iowa under Colonel John Scott on the left.

While they were moving into place, the rest of Banks's army and the wagons they had managed to save continued crossing the plain, trying to get as far east as possible before the Confederates appeared again. "The road to the front was seen to be filled with teams crowding to the rear," Scott reported later. "Evidences of past defeat and prospective retreat were everywhere visible. These were the moral surroundings as my command was moved to the extreme front and took position in the line of battle."

A Gap in the Line

To take advantage of the ridge the battery was on, Shaw moved the Twenty-Fourth Missouri forward to occupy it to the right of the battery. The move put his right beyond Dwight's support, but he considered it a better position than the one MacMillan's troops had occupied. Smith approved Shaw's movements except that he ordered him to move his main line even further to the right. That brought three companies of the Fourteenth Iowa (not specified) to the right of the Mansfield road and left a gap in the line of battle on Shaw's left. The right of the Fourteenth was immediately in the rear of the battery. Dwight's brigade ended up to the rear of the Fourteenth Iowa and nearly perpendicular to Shaw's line of battle.

Emory knew that Shaw was making the changes, Shaw wrote in his report, but to Shaw's knowledge Emory did not give any orders to adjust Dwight's location accordingly. In fact, he wrote, he did not see Emory again until after dark (after the battle was over).

"I had scarcely got into position when Dwight vacated his position and moved down to the right of the Mansfield road," Shaw wrote years later. "Some time after Dwight had abandoned his position on my right rear, Col. Benedict on my left moved to my rear . . . thus leaving my brigade entirely alone on the main road by which the enemy would approach, from one-fourth to one-half mile in advance of all other troops."

Taylor Arrives

In the meantime, the Confederates had followed them from the Sabine Crossroads battlefield. Major General Dick Taylor made his plans without knowing that the Sixteenth Corps had arrived; in fact, he was sure they were on the transports on the Red River with the Seventeenth. He thought he was facing only the troops he had defeated the day before, and he had five thousand new men. Brigadier General

Thomas James Churchill and Brigadier General Mosby M. Parsons had arrived from Arkansas and Missouri the night before with their divisions. They had marched twenty-two miles that day, but they had been allowed to rest until 2 a.m. before Taylor sent them off toward Pleasant Hill along with Major General John George Walker's and Brigadier General Camille J. Polignac's divisions. Taylor and his cavalry, commanded by Major General Thomas Green, left for Pleasant Hill a few hours later but were able to travel much faster than the men on foot.

When the first Confederate cavalry regiment arrived at Pleasant Hill, they found Banks's army in line of battle. Brigadier General Hamilton P. Bee, commanding the First Division, Green's Cavalry Corps, sent men out to see how far the line extended on each side and was surprised at "this extraordinary show of force on the part of the enemy after the occurrences of the previous day and the disastrous retreat of the night, except so far as to conclude that my irregular cavalry would have no business to charge such a line of battle." Taylor waited for Churchill's and Parsons's troops to reach them, and when they arrived in the afternoon, he gave them a couple of hours to rest. Then Taylor finalized his plans.

1. Churchill's and Parsons's Arkansas and Missouri divisions ("about 4,000 bayonets") with a couple of batteries would go to the right to outflank Benedict's brigade. Churchill would be the senior officer. They didn't know three of Smith's brigades were waiting behind Benedict's.
2. Churchill would push three of the cavalry regiments to the right. They were to head down the Jessup road twelve miles, take a cross road, and overtake Banks's retreat.
3. Walker would move through the woods to the right and attack by echelon of brigades from his right when he heard Churchill's and Parsons's guns.
4. Bee would wait on the Mansfield Road with Colonel Xavier Debray's and Colonel Augustus Buchel's cavalry and charge through Pleasant Hill when the attack on the right "disordered the enemy."
5. Left of the road, Green would be in charge. General James P. Major along with his own and most of Brigadier General Arthur P. Bagby's dismounted cavalry would move forward and outflank Shaw's brigade on its right. They didn't know Shaw's troops were fresh.
6. Polignac's division would wait in reserve.

"Thus it will be seen that my brigade was opposed to three brigades of cavalry under General Bee, Walker's division of infantry consisting of three brigades, and Polignac's division in reserve. . . . Walker also had three batteries," Shaw wrote later. He contrasted that with the forces facing the four brigades on the Federal left: Churchill's and Parsons's divisions of infantry, three regiments of cavalry, and two batteries.

Taylor estimated he had about 12,000 men at the time of the battle (same as the day before less casualties). Abstracts from returns and rosters show Banks had about 16,000 men present in the First Division and artillery of the Nineteenth Corps and in the First and Third Divisions of the Sixteenth Corps on March 31.

Confederate skirmishers appeared about midday, and all of Shaw's regiments threw out their own. The Fourteenth Iowa deployed Companies I and K. The Sixteenth and the Corps d'Afrique also had skirmishers in the woods on the left. Scattered skirmishing continued at different parts of the line all afternoon.

Shaw tried to find Dwight to ask him directly for support but couldn't find him or any of his staff. At about 3 p.m. the rebel skirmishers had passed Shaw's right and pressed his skirmishers so closely that it became necessary to support them with another company. Shaw again went in search of Dwight and this time found him. "After a great deal of difficulty," Shaw reported later, "he appeared to understand my position and promised to send the necessary support." (Dwight denied that in his report on the battle.) Instead, he withdrew farther to the rear without sending any support.

At about 4 p.m., Brigadier General Charles P. Stone, Banks's chief of staff, rode to the front. Shaw rode with him along his line showing him his changes and the necessity of a corresponding change in Dwight's line. Stone said he would see that his flanks were properly supported, according to Shaw. But no support came.

About the same time, Shaw wrote later, he saw that the rebels were moving their artillery into position on the left of the road in the edge of the forest and that the right of Walker's division had been moved forward so that Walker's line faced his line where it crossed the road. "I saw that an attack was imminent," he wrote. He sent word to his surgeon, Dr. G. M. Staples, to expect to start receiving the wounded within a half hour and to send forward ambulances and stretchers immediately.

Staples had taken one of the houses in the village for a hospital. According to Shaw, Banks rode up to the house and said he intended to use it as his headquarters for the night. When Staples told him about Shaw's orders, Banks replied, "Col. Shaw has had a little skirmishing with the enemy pickets, and he thinks he is going to have a fight. I assure you, Doctor, there will be no fighting tonight." Just then the Confederate artillery opened up. "Banks immediately rode rapidly away, and not in the direction of the firing," Shaw wrote.

Taylor Attacks

Three of Taylor's batteries began firing on the battery next to Shaw's brigade from the Confederates' right at about 4:30 p.m. "The Confederate artillery opened on us and seemed to have a good range on our line, for the shots took sad effect, the second shot killing two men of Co. B 14th Iowa," Major Hugo Hoffbauer recalled. "The men were ordered to lie down flat. . . . The battery on our right had all of their horses and a great many men killed."[91]

Shaw did not seem to consider that an excuse. The Twenty-Fifth New York Battery replied "feebly" for a few minutes, he wrote in his report afterward. He said they then "limbered up and

91. "Recollections of Red River Expedition."

disgracefully left the field," leaving a caisson and a gun on the road.

But the rebels soon began to realize Banks's army had more than one battery. "The rapidity and vigor evinced in the reply . . . from the Federal line was conclusive proof that we were about to attack an army other than the one encountered the day before," Bee wrote in his report afterward.

When the firing started, Dwight's brigade fell entirely out of Shaw's sight to the rear.

Taylor proceeded to put his plan into motion. Churchill and Parsons opened on the right, and Walker began his advance. Seeing the Twenty-Fifth New York battery being moved to the rear and hearing Churchill, Parsons, and Walker attacking on the Confederates' right, Green decided Banks's army was sufficiently "disordered" and ordered Bee forward. Debray's cavalry, followed by Buchel's cavalry and then the other mounted cavalries, were ready to charge past the Union line and through the town of Pleasant Hill as planned.

But Shaw was ready for them.

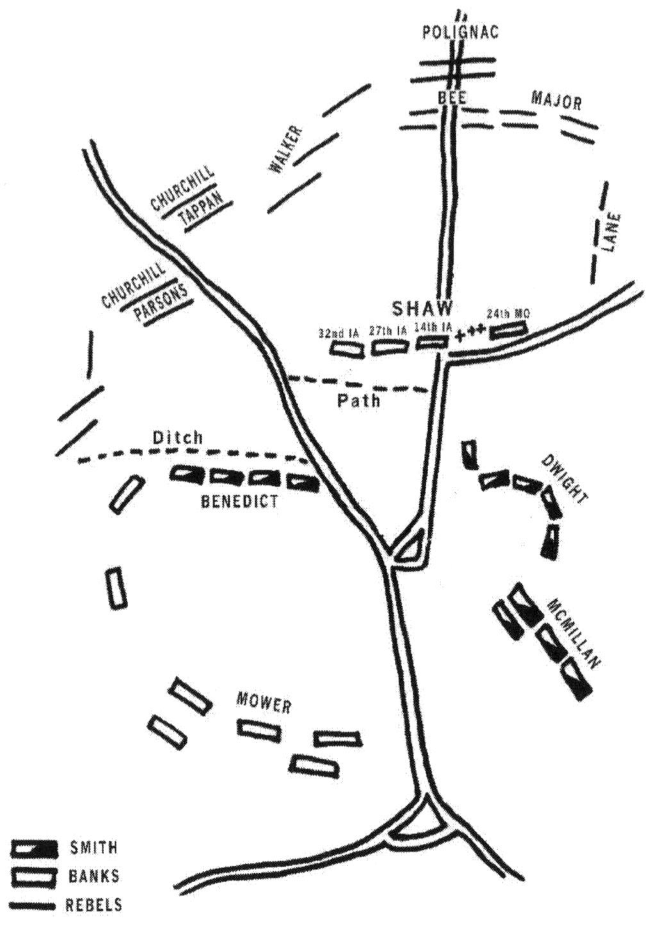

Map of Battle of Pleasant Hill by Lance Busch, after Col. William T. Shaw in "The Battle of Pleasant Hill," *The Annals of Iowa,* 1898.

> I was sitting upon my horse, with Col. Newbold, in front of the 14th Iowa in order to get a better view of the enemy's movements in the direction of the artillery firing. Col. Newbold called my attention to the formation of the cavalry across the road on the further side of the open ground.
>
> "I believe," he said, "that they are forming for a charge on our line."

Shaw rode along his line directing his regimental commanders to hold their fire until they had orders. His skirmishers were still on the right, and they had pushed forward into a clump of thick timber.

"There came a lull for a little while and then an order to prepare to receive a cavalry charge, but not to fire until the command was given," Hoffbauer wrote. "We raised and rested on one knee."

"We were ordered to fix bayonets," wrote John Ritland of the Thirty-Second Iowa in 1922, "and those in the front line dropped to their knees with their guns on the ground, while the line behind stood with guns to shoulders ready to press the bayonets home in the horses' breasts as they charged."[92]

An Awful Sight, an Imperishable Memory

The charge, in four columns, came down the Mansfield Road directly at the right center—the Fourteenth Iowa and Shaw's other regiments. Solon F. Benson of the Thirty-Second Iowa described the sight.

> A long line of mounted men issued from the opposite wood, and swept proudly across the great field. It was the Confederate brigade of General Bee men from western Texas, splendidly mounted and thoroughly disciplined. As they covered the long interval between the two lines of battle, they made a most magnificent display. They seemed to believe the Federal line had turned tail and left the field, the battery having almost ceased firing, and all being still on our side. Shaw's line was not easily seen lying close to the ground and screened by the woods in their immediate rear.

92. "The Civil War History of John Ritland" (Company K, Thirty-Second Iowa), originally published in the *Story City (Iowa) Herald* and *Roland (Iowa) Record* in 1922, http://www.ritland-32nd-iowa.com/index.shtml.

"The Rebel cavalry advanced toward the right and center, the exultant foe yelling in the most fiendish manner, at the same time brandishing their sabers in the air," reported the correspondent from the *New York Tribune*. "On they came at a slow trot in good order, as they neared our lines gradually quickening their pace."

Shaw's concealed skirmishers opened fire from the cavalry's left as it charged down the road and came into easy pistol range. The Fourteenth Iowa and Twenty-Fourth Missouri, in line across the road, held their fire until the cavalry was within 50 yards and then "literally annihilated them."

The *New York Tribune* correspondent wrote—

> As the cavalry dashed on at a gallop, each infantryman had selected his victim, and waiting till the three or four hundred were within about forty yards, the 14th Iowa regiment emptied nearly every saddle as quickly as though the order had been given to dismount.

"Horses and riders [were] rolling almost within our lines," Captain Warren C. Jones of the Fourteenth wrote in his report.

"Riders reeled and fell senseless. Horses were struck as dead as if a bolt of heaven had riven the very air. The scene was an appalling one," reported Gilbert. "Scarcely a man who made that charge but met with death."

The *New York Tribune* correspondent described the scene as "the awful reality of which the eye alone can describe to the soul."

> One of the wretches was badly wounded, and falling from his horse, his feet caught in the stirrup, frightening the horse which dashed off at a fearful speed, dragging the unfortunate Rebel after him until his head was entirely severed from his body, his brains being dashed upon the ground.

The reports on the Union side might have exaggerated the casualties, but Bee's report was similar.

> The empty saddles, the men shot and falling in all directions, the confusion produced a scene imperishable on my memory. Although the fire was now opened from the front as well as the ambuscade, what was left of Debray's gallant regiment succeeded in returning to our lines with a loss of one third of their number.

It was a scene that must have been "imperishable" on the memory of everyone who saw it. In 1915, Hoffbauer wrote, "When the smoke cleared away there were only two riders on horseback to be seen. It was certainly a terrible sight to look upon the dead and wounded before us."

"They came on at a terrible rate, and though halted appreciably by our formidable front, they plunged through," Ritland wrote.

> It was an awful sight to see the number of dead and wounded scattered about, as well as the poor horses staggering around bleeding to death or galloping frantically about with saddles and straps flying.

Although "all went rearwards in the wildest confusion," Benson wrote, not many were actually unhorsed. Those who did not fall to the brigade's fire dismounted and hid among the ravines and small pines.

> Once within the shelter of the woods beyond the open field, they dismounted and returned immediately as infantry, and advancing upon Shaw's line, they poured volley after volley into his ranks. Our men believed they were fresh troops, and that the cavalry had been utterly destroyed. But every battle is essentially a series of illusions and this was one of them.

Buchel saw what was happening in time to pull back his cavalry. He moved to the Confederates' left, had his men dismount, and attacked Shaw's brigade from there. Buchel was mortally wounded during this part of the battle, falling within the lines of the Fourteenth Iowa. Bee also moved to the left, had the rest of the cavalries dismount, and fought alongside Major's dismounted cavalry under Green.

The Rest of Taylor's Plan

Churchill's division's attacks on the left side of Banks's line were continuing. The rebel troops pushed Benedict's brigade back and through Smith's line behind it.

Walker's troops advanced in two lines diagonally across the field by echelon of brigades from his right. His first brigade struck the unprotected left flank Shaw had been worried about, the Thirty-Second Iowa. As with the cavalry, Shaw's troops waited until they were close before firing. Walker's second and third brigades attacked successively a couple of the regiments of Shaw's brigade: the Twenty-Seventh Iowa and seven companies (not specified) of the Fourteenth Iowa.

In Smith's words, "the battle immediately became general."

In Taylor's words, "The stubborn resistance offered by the enemy along the whole line soon convinced me that he had received re-enforcements of fresh troops."

As the rebels crossed the field toward Shaw's brigade, they were "shouting an indescribable battle cry, which would cause the nerves of the timid to vibrate, reminding one of all the ferocity of savages," the *New York Tribune* correspondent reported. Shaw's men kept up a steady fire that soon sent the Confederates' first line to fall back in disorder. The *New York Tribune* correspondent described it.

> There arose from the crouching forms of several thousand loyal men a fearful roll of musketry, opening wide gaps in the Rebel lines; but they were as spedily [*sic*] closed, and the enraged foe with a sudden dash threw his gigantic force against our front, and for a moment our whole line seemed to waver, giving way a few yards.
>
> The suspense of this fearful moment was terrible to bear, for it did seem to portend defeat. In another moment our artillery scattered grape and cannister in appaling [*sic*] quantities upon the exasperated enemy, literally mowing them down as with an enormous scythe.

But the Confederates started to take advantage of the gap between the Thirty-Second Iowa's left and Benedict's brigade—the gap that Shaw had begged for more troops to fill before the battle started. The regiment's fire was so destructive, the Thirty-Second's commander reported later, that the rebels "faltered, passed to my left through the open space, and to my rear losing heavily by the fire of my left wing as he passed, but threatening to cut off my command from our main forces." Scott had to change his front to face the danger on his flank and rear.

Meanwhile, Major's troops continued attacking the Twenty-Fourth Missouri and the other three companies (not specified) of the Fourteenth Iowa on Shaw's right, the other flank Shaw had tried to obtain protection for before the battle.

"Again and again did the enemy press our front, and we fought each other at 15 paces. Every effort made by them resulted in their discomfiture," Fyan, commanding officer of the Twenty-Fourth Missouri, wrote in his report. "At length they appeared upon our right flank in force, and poured volley after volley upon us."

"The rattle of musketry was incessant and deafening," Gilbert reported. Jones wrote that "the enemy was repulsed in front with a heavy slaughter." "The roar of battle drowning every other sound, guns heated until it was dangerous to load, smoke covering the whole field until neither friend nor foe could be seen," Benson wrote.

"The fighting was close and hot," Colonel George Wythe Baylor, a member of the Confederate's dismounted cavalry, wrote in his report of the battle. Shaw's brigade "had a very strong position."

> The pine logs and rails of which I have spoken were piled up at a right angle with the main road. Behind this the enemy were lying, and could only be shot when in the act of firing. Across a small enclosure and in rear of this temporary work was an abrupt hollow running parallel with it, where the enemy were securely posted in heavy numbers. We were not strong enough to dislodge them or flank them.

They fought with more than guns; Walker had given orders to rely on the bayonet to save time and ammunition. Taylor wrote in his report of the battle that "these orders were well carried out as many ghastly wounds among the federals testify."

Retreat!

The rebels were able to move between Shaw's brigade and the rest of Smith's forces, separating them, and the fighting extended a mile behind Shaw's line and into the town. Smith sent orders to Shaw to fall back so the two lines could join; Smith knew the Confederates were getting in Shaw's rear, but Shaw didn't realize it yet.

Shaw, however, was too busy fighting to retreat. "At this time I was very heavily engaged along my whole line with Walker's division of infantry and Major's dismounted cavalry," he wrote later. "I told Capt. Lyons to say to Gen. Smith that I was so heavily engaged I could not then fall back without great danger, owing to the heavy timber in the rear of three of my regiments and the fierce attack in front; that as soon as I repulsed the present attack I would comply with his order."

"I soon repulsed the enemy along my whole line," Shaw wrote later. "It was now getting dark, and I commenced the withdrawing of my brigade." He had dispatched all his staff officers to request support, so he had to deliver the order to withdraw himself. He rode from the right to the left behind the line giving the order. The brush and timber were so thick he could scarcely see ten paces. As he approached the rear of the regiment farthest to the left of his brigade, the Thirty-Second Iowa, he discovered the Confederate forces that were retreating before Smith's line. He had to leave Scott to act without orders.

Returning to the far right, he found the Twenty-Fourth Missouri had had to change its front because of the attack from its right. "Exposed as the regiment was to a heavy cross-fire against such numbers I ordered them to fall back, which they did disputing every foot," Fyan wrote. The Confederates had overwhelming numbers at the brigade's front, and the Fourteenth Iowa and Twenty-Fourth Missouri were nearly out of ammunition.

When the Twenty-Fourth Missouri fell back, the Fourteenth, which had been to its left, had to change direction to meet the rebels on the right. The commanding officer, Newbold, had been killed in the crossfire, falling from his horse mortally wounded. A ball had passed through his body from the right breast into his left arm. Four lieutenants were killed as well. Captain Warren C. Jones had assumed command.

Shaw re-formed his brigade on the ground Dwight had occupied behind him; Dwight immediately fell back farther and out of sight again.

Smith's Charge

In the meantime, the rebels' right had advanced beyond Smith's left and were "taken in flank and rolled up" by Lynch's brigade. "Seizing the opportunity," Smith reported, "I ordered a charge by the whole line."

"Southern soldiers now stood where Shaw's line had been," Benson summarized, "and a great southern army filled the whole center of the field."

> But they had gone a little too far, and the tip of the crescent's left horn charged their right flank, and McMillan charged their left, and the whole line of Smith's great crescent, rising up from the ground like an apparition delivered their fire, and with a great, prolonged cheer, charged straight at the southern line.

Captain Charles T. Granger of the Twenty-Seventh Iowa, acting assistant adjutant general on Shaw's staff, saw the charge when he returned from carrying the request for support to Smith (after trying to find Dwight first).

> I witnessed a signal and gallant military feat not falling to the lot of every volunteer soldier.

> The enemy came forward flushed with the prospect, and their shouts gave evidence that the victory was theirs. And so it seemed to the observer who knew not what they were at once to encounter. They came up a gradual slope and when just at its top, as if from out of the earth, rose Gen. Mower's command of the Sixteenth Army Corps, and with a volley and a charge, and in much less time than I can state the facts, it put that line, so confident a moment before, in full retreat and with results so well known to history.
>
> Had not the main body of Taylor's army been held in check by our brigade no such feat would have been possible.

Watching from a high spot on the left, the *New York Tribune* correspondent observed—

> The sun shone directly in the faces of our men while the wind blew back the smoke of both the enemy's fire and that of our own gallant men into our ranks, rendering it almost impossible at times to distinguish the enemy in the dense clouds of smoke.

Left alone in the center of the battlefield, fighting on his front and on the Thirty-Second Iowa's left flank, Scott suddenly discovered that three of his companies—part of his right wing—had been withdrawn and that two of his company commanders had been killed. He was not aware of this earlier because the timber and undergrowth kept him from seeing his entire line at once. He set up a new line on the right and was now fighting in three directions. His regiment could have been taken by the rebels if they had decided to close in, but they were forced back on the left and retreated from his front at sunset. The fight still raged to his rear, but finally Scott was able to move about two hundred yards to the left and rear, where he and his men met and joined Smith's troops. They were nearly out of ammunition.

"We drove them back," Smith wrote triumphantly, "desperately fighting, step by step across the field, through the wood, and into the open field beyond, fully a mile from the battlefield, when they took advantage of the darkness and fell back toward Mansfield thoroughly whipped and demoralized."

The *New York Tribune's* correspondent described the end of the battle.

> As the dusk of evening became more and more intense, and the last glimmering streaks of day were rapidly fading away, the enemy struggled fiercely for the possession of the

> battlefield, and a tremendous roar of musketry burst forth from their staggering lines, which was responded to by two or three terrific volleys from our side, and then came that dead, quiet calm, broken only by the moaning of our men's voices and the groans of the dying.

According to Smith, just after his final charge Banks rode up to him, shook his hand, and told him, "God bless you, general; you have saved the army."

Tending the injured after battle, *Harper's Weekly,* July 12, 1862.

CHAPTER 5

AFTER PLEASANT HILL: COMPELLED TO RETREAT FROM A RETREATING FOE

Complying with Brigadier General A. J. Smith's command, Colonel William T. Shaw withdrew his brigade from the Pleasant Hill line of battle as darkness began to fall. The men held their ground until he ordered them to retreat, he reported later. The thick brush caused some temporary confusion, but the troops rapidly re-formed in the rear and were soon ready again to meet the rebels. Confederate Major General Dick Taylor's forces "had been driven from the field on their right and had now retired on their left" (on Shaw's side), Solon F. Benson of the Thirty-Second Iowa wrote later. Smith had his Army of the Tennessee detachment, including Shaw's brigade, bivouac in line on the field of battle, ready to resume fighting at daylight. The men would have been surrounded by the sights, sounds, and smells of the dead and dying men and horses.[93]

Taylor wrote his report of the battle April 18, 1864.

> We had driven them at every point, and but for the mistake and consequent confusion on the right we would have captured most of his army. . . . After order was restored I directed the infantry to fall back some 6 miles to water, as there was none to be had nearer and all were parched with thirst. As many of the cavalry as could be foraged were sent to the same point, where forage and rations had been accumulated. The remainder, except Debray's regiment, was ordered to Mansfield to feed and rest. This was absolutely necessary. The cavalry had been fighting and marching for four consecutive days, and man and horse had been without food for forty hours.

However, he wrote, "I remained with General Bee some 300 yards from the battle-field, two companies of Debray's regiment picketing on the field. The noise of wagons moving in the rear of

93. Unless otherwise noted, the sources for this chapter are Appendix E in *Report of Adjutant General, 1865–1866*; Benson, "Battle of Pleasant Hill"; Shaw, "Battle of Pleasant Hill"; and R. Scott, "Operations in Louisiana and Trans-Mississippi," 162–638.

the enemy's position confirmed my opinion that he would retreat in the night."

Taylor was right. At about midnight, Smith received orders from Major General Nathaniel Banks to have his command ready to move at two o'clock in the morning. He was to withdraw silently from the field and follow the Nineteenth Army Corps back to Grand Ecore, "making such dispositions of [his] troops and trains as would enable [him] to repel an attack on the rear of the column." Smith did not mention it in his report, but the *New York Tribune* correspondent ("Battles in Louisiana") reported that all the officers of the Sixteenth Corps argued in favor of going after the Confederate army and pressing on to Mansfield the next day.

Banks's justification for his decision to go back to Grand Ecore, which had been made before the battle started and which was the same as Taylor's reason for having his men fall back at the end of the day, was the lack of food and water at the site. The army's provisions had been on the supply wagons Banks had sent back that morning, and the local wells had been exhausted.[94]

94. "Battles in Louisiana."

The Abandoned

Smith pointed out to Banks that the dead of his command were not buried and that he had no way to transport his wounded. In fact, many of the wounded had not even been removed from the battlefield yet. Smith requested permission to remain until noon the next day to give him an opportunity to bury his dead and provide for the wounded as well as possible. Banks refused permission.

The pain at having to leave the dead and wounded unattended was especially evident in the report of Colonel John Scott, commander of the Thirty-Second Iowa in Shaw's brigade. His losses had been the greatest; he later reported the Thirty-Second Iowa had 210 killed, wounded, and missing in the battle.

> It was not practicable to give any attention to the wounded until about midnight, at which time parties were sent for that purpose, but were not permitted to pass our lines. This was the more readily acquiesced in under the belief that we could care for them in the morning. At 3 o clock A.M., we were astounded at being ordered into line, and bring up the rear, our army already gone, and the advance of our

forces, which had left after the battle, being then some miles distant.

"There is a degree of uncertainty in relation to the casualties that is extremely embarrassing and painful," he wrote in his report, his bitterness apparent. "I fear the number of fatal casualties will exceed the number stated and that of those marked missing many are killed or wounded. From an early period of the action our position was such that disabled men seeking the hospital would necessarily fall into the hands of the enemy in our rear."

He added these comments to the history he later wrote of the Thirty-Second Iowa:

> When the attack was made on the 32d Iowa Infantry it was known to me that we were in reality the rear of a retreating army, and not the front of a fighting army, which we should have been.
>
> The battle closed as darkness settled upon the field, leaving us in possession of every part of it except the first position of our brigade. The enemy had fought, first with confidence, elated over his success of the day previous, then with desperation, to hold positions he had gained at heavy loss. He was driven from the field terribly punished for the temerity

> and recklessness with which he had advanced, demoralized, his columns broken, and many of his troops in panic and rout.
>
> This was a defeat, but a defeat only to our foe. The stake fought for *by him* was the Trans-Mississippi Empire; by our commanding General, the safe retreat of his army. We won both; abandoned the former to the enemy *after he had retreated* and gave to a brilliant victory all the moral results of a defeat. Finally, the Thirty-second Iowa Infantry blushes to place upon its banner the name of a field where its dead and wounded were cruelly abandoned to an enemy, who, many hours afterward, humbly asked leave to care for his own!

Banks's report, however, assured General Ulysses S. Grant he had done the opposite of what Smith, Scott, and other officers accused him of.

> The wounded were gathered from the battlefield, placed in comfortable hospitals, and left under the care of competent surgeons and assistants. The dead remaining on the battlefield, as far as possible, were buried during the night. The next day medical supplies and provisions, with competent attendants, were sent in.

"As far as possible" could mean anything regarding the burials, but some of the wounded soldiers would differ with Banks regarding the wounded. Ben Van Dyke, a member of the Fourteenth Iowa's Company D, was shot in the thigh during the battle, and he lay on the battlefield for the rest of the battle and throughout the night afterward.

> Finally night put an end to the fighting, and we fondly hoped that now we should be gathered up and receive medical aid. But the Union army marched away, and there we lay all night among the dead and wounded, the latter calling piteously for water and help. . . .
>
> The long night after the battle finally wore away, and the bright sun rose on the beautiful morning of Sunday, April 10th, with the dead and wounded yet uncared for.
>
> About 10 o'clock A. M. the rebel army, discovering the retreat of the union army, came following them up. And these southern men gathered us up and conveyed us about two miles east of Pleasant Hill, to a country place where our people had established a hospital the previous day, and there we remained as prisoners of war.

> At that place we found surgeons from both armies, and they were amputating arms and legs, almost by the wagon load.

Solon Benson was another of the wounded soldiers left behind; he lost his arm either at the time or by amputation afterward. He wrote a first-hand account in 1906 of the care he and the others received (and didn't receive). The Federal army left "the most badly wounded, some in the several improvised hospitals, and others scattered over the great field uncared for," he wrote.

> The dead lay scattered over the field unburied. Five surgeons and a very few attendants remained to care for the wounded, and the public buildings, the great Childers Mansion, and some other buildings were transformed into temporary hospitals, and filled to overflowing with the wounded. A camp near a country house two miles east of town received "the overflow." . . .
>
> All night the surgeons labored with the wounded, and when the bright Sabbath sun rose on the morning of the 10th, the army had disappeared, and that little town of less than one hundred souls found itself oppressed with seven times its number of wounded men belonging to both armies. And in their haste

the army had taken away everything needed for the comfort of the men. There were neither provisions nor medical supplies.

The *New York Times* said Banks sent a supply of medical and sanitary stores by flag of truce immediately after the battle and Taylor delivered them to the surgeons. Benson wrote that Banks sent two army wagons full of medical supplies in charge of the Nineteenth's medical director four days later. However, many of the wounded men Banks left behind at Pleasant Hill died.[95]

Benson said Banks left four hundred wounded soldiers and more than half died. A *New York Tribune* correspondent, however, said the Army left about five hundred men who had been wounded at Mansfield and Pleasant Hill and about 160 of them died in Pleasant Hill.[96]

Van Dyke expected the wounded would go from there to a military prison, so he escaped from the hospital at the end of April. Traveling by foot and pretending to be a rebel soldier for much

95. "Our Wounded at Sabine Cross-Roads," *New York Times,* June 30, 1864, https://www.nytimes.com/1864/06/30/archives/from-neworleans-our-wounded-at-sabine-crossroads.html.

96. "Return of Three Hundred Wounded Soldiers—Humane Treatment from the Rebels. Correspondence of the New York Tribune." *Weekly National Intelligencer,* Washington, D.C., July 7, 1864.

of the journey, he managed to rejoin the Fourteenth Iowa at Yellow Bayou on May 18.

The Confederates paroled about three hundred of the surviving wounded men in June. The remaining ones who had "sufficiently recovered" went to Camp Ford, the Confederate prison camp near Tyler, Texas. George Campbell of the Fourteenth's Company B was among them. They were there until June of the following year, soon after the war ended but months after the Fourteenth Iowa was mustered out.[97]

Who Won?

"The morning of the 10th found us in possession of Pleasant Hill, the enemy retreating secretly in the night leaving his dead unburied and some 400 wounded in our hands," Taylor reported, and there has never been agreement since on which side won the battle. Taylor's forces were in retreat at the end of the battle. However, Banks retreated as well a few hours later, and as a result the Confederates ended up in possession of the battlefield.

"It is said that the Battle of Pleasant Hill, April 9th, 1864, bears the unique distinction of an engagement from which both belligerents fled

97. "Return of Three Hundred Wounded Soldiers"; Thrift, *Roster and Record,* 755–781.

precipitately, and yet each party claimed the victory as soon as it discovered the flight of the other," Benson wrote in 1906. Little has changed since. As of this writing, the Wikipedia page for the battle says the battle of Pleasant Hill was a Confederate win in the summary and a Federal win in the text. The National Park Service summary says it was a Union victory[98] while some southern history sites say the rebels won.

"It is universally supposed," the *New York Tribune* correspondent wrote in the conclusion of his article, "and I am not prepared to deny its correctness, that we inflicted a heavier loss of life upon the enemy on Saturday."

> The undiminished valor of our troops forced the enemy to retreat, leaving us in full possession of the battle-field. Did we carefully bury our dead, and gather up the thousands of rifles that were thrown upon the field? No; we stole off stealthily before daylight Sunday morning, Gen. A. J. Smith's forces covering our retreat, with 500 cavalry as a rear guard, under the command of Col. Lucas.

98. National Park Service, "Battle Detail: Pleasant Hill," https://www.nps.gov/civilwar/search-battles-detail.htm?battleCode=LA019.

Confederate Lieutenant General E. Kirby Smith, who did not arrive from Shreveport until after the battle was over, wrote twenty years later that Banks turned what could have been a victory into defeat.[99]

> Our troops attacked with vigor and at first with success, but, exposing their right flank, were finally repulsed and thrown into confusion. The Missouri and Arkansas troops, with a brigade of Walker's division, were broken and scattered. The enemy recovered cannon which we had captured the day before, and two of our pieces with the dead and wounded were left on the field. Our repulse at Pleasant Hill was so complete and our command was so disorganized that had Banks followed up his success vigorously he would have met but feeble opposition to his advance on Shreveport.
>
> . . . [I] was consulting with General Taylor when some stragglers from the battle-field, where our wounded were still lying, brought the intelligence that Banks had precipitately retreated after the battle, converting a victory which he might have claimed into a defeat.

99. Kirby Smith in Robert Underwood Johnson and Clarence Clough Buel, eds., "Defense of Red River" in *Battles and Leaders of the Civil War,* 372.

> Our troops in rear rallied and the field was next day occupied by us. . . . Our troops were completely paralyzed and disorganized by the repulse at Pleasant Hill. . . . Before we could reorganize at Mansfield and get into condition to advance over the fifty-five miles of wilderness that separated our armies, the enemy had been reenforced and intrenched at Grand Ecore.

Regardless, Taylor's report at the time says, "Thus was defeated this great expedition for the conquest of the Trans-Mississippi Department. The third army of the enemy in point of numbers on the theater of the war was routed and driven from the field."

He was right. After the defeat at Sabine Crossroads and the retreat from Pleasant Hill, Banks abandoned the plan of capturing Shreveport. That was the end of the Louisiana phase of the Red River Campaign.

Casualties

The statistics for the losses of the five brigades of the Sixteenth Corps were 98 killed, 540 wounded, and 115 missing (totaling 753). The number of killed included 10 officers, 8 of whom were in Shaw's brigade and 5 of whom were in the

Fourteenth Iowa. Of the 59 deaths of enlisted men in Shaw's brigade, the Thirty-Second Iowa had 33, more than twice as many as the Fourteenth's 14 deaths. Similarly, of 326 total wounded in Shaw's brigade, 115 were in the Thirty-Second and 61 were in the Fourteenth.

Among the replacement companies of the Fourteenth Iowa, Hiram Aurner, Joseph R. Leyle, Edward O'Brien, and Sydney Parker of Company B and John Gambell of Company C were killed. Gambell was one of the Columbus men who had enlisted a few months earlier. Meroni Clark of Company B was wounded in the battle and taken prisoner, and he died of his wounds at the Confederate prison camp in Texas July 15, 1864.[100]

The wounded of the new Company A were John Gorman, Francis McKean, David Morrison, David Sloper, Charles Sweeney, George Turner, and George W. Zink. In Company B, George Campbell, Stephen M. Dicken, William H. George, Allen E. Holmes, Winfield S. Kingsbury, Alexander F. Nicol, and William W. Parmenter were wounded. In Company C, John Myers was wounded and Myron Roberts was both wounded and taken prisoner. Henry Meier of Company B also was taken prisoner. Charles C. Smith, who

100. Thrift, *Roster and Record,* 755–781.

had enlisted in Company A at Fort Halleck in November, was listed as missing but had deserted the day before the battle.[101]

Emory lost 501 killed, wounded, and missing from his three brigades of the Nineteenth Corps.[102] The numbers for both corps total 1,254 Federal casualties. However, the National Park Service estimates 1,369 casualties for the Union and 1,626 for the Confederates, and the American Battlefield Protection Program says they were 1,100 and 2,000 respectively.[103]

Bitter Troops

The criticism of Banks's handling of Sabine Crossroads and Pleasant Hill was nearly unanimous (with one exception being the *New York Times* June 30 account of the battle). An anonymous letter published in the *Pittsburgh Daily Commercial* (and elsewhere) says, "Officers and men blame each other, and unite in saying that it was a most miserable and criminal piece of

---

101. Thrift, *Roster and Record,* 755–781.

102. Emory in Scott, 393. Note: The return of casualties for the Nineteenth in the *War of the Rebellion* includes those from the day before.

103. National Park Service, "Battle Detail: Pleasant Hill"; American Battlefield Protection Program, "CWSAC Battle Summaries: Pleasant Hill," http://nps.gov/abpp/battles/la019.htm.

generalship. Brig. Gen. A. J. Smith must be excepted altogether from condemnation. His men fought like tigers."[104]

John Ritland of the Thirty-Second Iowa wrote in 1922 that Banks was "a traitor who had arranged it so that we were bound to lose. He let a few detachments bear the front of battle, while the main army lay inactive."

An unsigned letter to the editor of the *Burlington (Iowa) Weekly Hawk-Eye* dated May 17, 1864, was scornful.

> Gen. Banks, as a military genius, is not very highly appreciated by the officers and men of this department, and especially the men of this expedition, who say they believe that if he had had twice as large an army as he had, he would have gotten them all "gobbled" [captured]. And their eyes fairly flash with indignation when they tell of being compelled by orders to retreat from a retreating foe, which they say was the case at Pleasant Hill, and which was corroborated by some of our men who were taken prisoner in the fight and afterwards escaped, who said that the rebels

104. "The Battles of Red River," *Pittsburgh Daily Commercial,* April 29, 1864.

retreated eighteen miles before they halted their columns.[105]

Thirty-Second Iowa quartermaster T. C. McCall expressed his anger in his letter to the *Iowa State Register.*[106]

> But the most bitter part of the whole affair was that after we had fairly whipped the rebels and driven them from the field, we disgracefully fell back (or rather retreated) leaving our dead and wounded to the mercy of our enemies. We have learned satisfactorily that one regiment of rebel cavalry was so badly routed that they never stopped till they reached Mansfield, some twenty miles distant; and that two divisions of their infantry were so panic-stricken that they never halted until they were six miles from the field—and that the entire rebel army except their pickets fell back six miles that night.[107]

105. "From Louisiana," June 18, 1864.

106. Written April 16, 1864, and published May 14, 1864.

107. McCall in Shaw, "The Battle of Pleasant Hill," 423.

Shaw's Fury

Shaw was furious about the losses in his brigade—which he blamed on the failure of his fellow officers to provide the support they promised for his flanks—and about the orders to leave the battlefield.

> The long list of killed and wounded amounting to nearly 500 shows the desperate valor with which my men fought. My men were the first in the fight, the longest in the fight, and in the hardest of the fight and were the last to leave the battle field and were ready and willing to remain and reap the fruits of a victory which they had so dearly purchased, but they were soldiers and must obey the orders of their superiors.

Scott's report, as published in *Report of the Adjutant General and Acting Quartermaster General of the State of Iowa* in 1866, contains these excerpts from an undated letter he says Shaw wrote (called a "statement" in the index):

> Although I had less than one-tenth of the force on the field, my loss was full one-half of the whole loss of that day, being about five hundred killed and wounded out of seventeen hundred; and yet my brigade was considered

in such good condition as to be ordered to cover the retreat of the army to Grand Ecore that night, and the next day. The loss in the 32d Iowa alone was equal to the whole loss in Banks's army; it wanted but few of being equal to the loss in all of Smith's forces outside of my brigade. The loss in the four Iowa regiments was equal to the whole loss of all the forces outside of my brigade; and yet, with these facts, the name of Iowa is not mentioned in any report of the battle I have yet seen in the New Orleans papers.

But, it may be suggested that the loss does not show the extent of the fighting. In this instance, at least, it is a fair index. I was engaged with the enemy for over seven hours, while no other forces were under fire one hour. I was under a heavy and destructive artillery fire forty-five minutes before a gun was fired upon any other part of the field. I received and repulsed a heavy charge of cavalry, followed by an attack of infantry which I also repulsed, before a gun was fired upon any other part of our line. My loss was all in fair fight, in good position, well protected, except my flanks, and no man moved to the rear till he was ordered; and I gave no such orders till I received them from my superiors. That order would never have been necessary had it not been for

> [Brigadier Generals William Dwight and William H. Emory].

Shaw then proceeded to accuse Emory, Dwight, and Brigadier General James W. McMillan of being drunk on the battlefield and accused Emory and Dwight of being cowards as well.

> I have heard that it was a great battle, fought by fifteen or twenty thousand men on our side, with two Major-Generals and a dozen Brigadiers, more or less; and I know that about one-half the fighting was done by a single brigade of some seventeen hundred men, without artillery, and that brigade was a quarter of a mile in advance of all other troops.

He was angry about the unexpected command to leave the battlefield and cover the retreat to Grand Ecore in the middle of the night too.

> At dark we had whipped them at every point, and driven them back in utter confusion, but our lines were drawn in, our dead, and part of our wounded, were left on the field. At 1 o'clock, A.M., the Army of the Gulf began its grand retreat. Being a little foot-sore, it took a couple of hours start of Smith's forces, which

> started at three. But as the Second Brigade had thrashed about one-half the rebel army and only lost five hundred men out of seventeen hundred, it might reasonably be expected that the remaining twelve hundred could "clean out" the other half if they should attempt to interfere with the grand retreat of the Great General!

Shaw's letter (or statement) would become important later in the year when his superiors punished him for expressing his opinions, but information about it is scarce. Books published in 1865 by Addison A. Stuart and in 1866 by Lurton Dunham Ingersoll quote Shaw's remarks and say they were in a published letter and do not mention Scott's report (which was not published until 1866). Stuart says it was published in the *Dubuque (Iowa) Times,* and Ingersoll says it was in the *Anamosa (Iowa) Eureka.* The letter does not appear in a search of the *Eureka,* and the author was not able to search the *Times* for this period.

Another letter Shaw wrote May 23 to the editor of the *Eureka* begins "I sent you an account of our Pleasant Hill fight, but I am afraid you did not get it, as about that time our mail got captured. I will, however, send you soon my official report." The *Eureka* published the May 23 letter (which described the encounter at Bayou des Glaises on May 18) on June 10 with an editor's note saying, "The letter mentioned by Col. Shaw, giving an account of the fight at Pleasant Hill, did not come to hand. It was doubtless in the captured mail."

It is possible copies of Shaw's letter about the battle circulated for a while without being published anywhere except the books mentioned earlier. Another possibility is hinted at in a letter written in reply to Shaw's May 23 letter. J. T. Summers, Twenty-Eighth Iowa chaplain, was offended by Shaw's general criticism of Banks's army in that letter because he felt it applied to his and other regiments unfairly, and he issued what sounds like a threat.[108]

> The Colonel starts out by saying that he had sent a communication that was captured. We saw a letter picked up by an officer at the rebel distributing office on the Red River expedition which was somewhat mutilated, but which must have furnished some good food for rebels, and if for shame's sake the Colonel will not deny his own signature, he can learn something of its fate by calling at this office.

108. "Misrepresentations of Iowa Regiments in the Field," *Davenport (Iowa) Daily Gazette,* July 21, 1864.

Shaw submitted a copy of his official report of the battle, dated April 15, 1864, to the *Eureka* as promised, and it was published there on June 24.[109] The official report hints that Dwight and Emory were drunk, saying that some officers had seen a drunken man they believed was Dwight and that Shaw didn't see Emory until after the fighting had ended. An editor's note in the same issue was more specific without naming the source.

> We will say here that we have it on very good authority that Gen's. McMillan, Emory and Dwight were all drunk during this battle—so drunk they could not ride their horses. They ought to be decapitated forthwith as ignominious cowards and vile wretches for being drunk at a moment of such peril to so many thousands of brave men.

No matter what really happened, the accusations that certain officers were drunk at the battle of Pleasant Hill appeared in print in association with Shaw's name and would become significant by fall.

---

109. "Battle of Pleasant Hill: Official Report of Col. Wm. T. Shaw."

Dam built on Red River to raise the water level enough for Major General Nathaniel Banks's boats to pass through. George Slater, *Harper's Weekly,* June 18, 1864 (Digital Public Library of America).

CHAPTER 6
BANKS'S RETREAT:
40 DAYS OF CONTINUAL SKIRMISHING

Valentine Spawr left Pleasant Hill with a sore throat and cough. "Soon after the return of my company from the battle of Pleasant Hill on Red River in Louisiana I noticed that he was troubled with a cough & he complained very much of his throat and lungs," fellow soldier Herman A. Miles wrote in an affidavit for Spawr's widow's pension application in 1886. Spawr was a good singer before then, fellow soldier Myron L. Roberts said in an affidavit in 1884. He "used to sing a great deal for the boys but during the winter and spring of 64 we were on the march a good deal and were subject to a great deal of exposure much of the time. He could not sing for us on account of his throat and lungs troubling him."

The Sixteenth Corps marched twenty miles April 10, the day after the battle of Pleasant Hill, and got back to Grand Ecore April 11. The troops made camp on the bluffs about a mile above the town and waited for the return of the fleet that was supposed to travel by river to Shreveport. They foraged for food in the countryside, dug entrenchments, felled timber, and generally prepared for Confederate Major General Dick Taylor's army to attack.[110]

When the fleet wasn't back by April 13, two brigades, with Colonel William T. Shaw's in the lead, started up the river to look for it. They marched about twelve miles that evening and camped a few miles above Campti. Brigadier General A. J. Smith, commander of the detachment from the Army of the Tennessee, reported that they "met a portion of the fleet there, they having by energy, good judgment, and rare good fortune succeeded in running the batteries and land forces of the enemy without the loss of a boat, though some were completely riddled with shot." They returned to Grand Ecore the next day.

Continuous Fighting on Flanks and Rear

Another Orville Burke letter to the editor of the *Anamosa (Iowa) Eureka* describes the Fourteenth Iowa's travels during the rest of April and May. After the battle of Pleasant Hill, he wrote, "the

110. Unless otherwise noted, the sources of the information this chapter are Appendix E in *Report of Adjutant General, 1865–1866* and R. Scott, "Operations in Louisiana and Trans-Mississippi," 162–638.

retreat commenced, the result of which was encouragement to the rebels and continuous fighting on our rear and flanks for six consecutive weeks."[111]

Major General Nathaniel Banks resumed his retreat April 20. The first day, he had Smith's command move four miles from Grand Ecore to Natchitoches to be the *point de resistance* while Banks's other troops passed between them and the river. The next day they had to wait for the rest of Banks's army to pass before they fell in at the rear that evening. "The result of this was, that on the morning of the 22d, after a night on the road, we were scarcely a mile from our camp the day previous, but more harassed and exhausted than we would have been under a fair march," Colonel John Scott, commander of the Thirty-Second Iowa, wrote.

"The enemy pushed the pursuit vigorously," Smith wrote. "The rear was skirmishing every day and nearly all day. Twice during the march we were forced to form line and teach them a lesson."

Burke described the weariness of the soldiers when they reached Isle Brevelle at the end of the day April 22.

111. "From the 14th Iowa Infantry," July 1, 1864.

> We left Natchitoches about 12 o'clock at night and marched till 2 o'clock the next night, a distance of about fifty miles, and then laid down upon the hard ground, many of us without blankets, and too near tired out to make any kind of a bed, but down in the road thousands of us lay in the dust just where we had made a halt.

Scott wrote that they marched twenty-five miles that day; modern maps show the distance between Natchitoches and Isle Breville to be about ten miles. It probably felt like twenty-five or fifty miles.

The next day, April 23, they advanced south again but made only five miles because of delays in the front and attacks on the rear. At about 3 a.m. on April 24, the rebels began to shell their camp from the rear, and at sunrise about three or four thousand attacked. The Seventeenth Corps was in the extreme rear and repulsed the attack. The command then moved on to Cotile, where they arrived at about 10 p.m.

It was about twenty-eight miles from there to Alexandria, according to Scott. They traveled there the next two days, "the enemy hovering about, picking up stragglers, and making insolent demonstrations," he wrote. The Fourteenth Iowa, at the rear, arrived in Alexandria the afternoon of

April 26; the head of the column had reached it the day before. "We endeavored to get some rest and brush off the dust," Burke wrote, "but before the din of battle had scarcely left our ears, the long roll was beaten and we were collected into line of battle again and marched out."

Demoralizing Orders

They spent the next couple of weeks in the area of Alexandria while the army worked on getting the gunboats over the falls of the Red River. Spawr's duties might have been lightened somewhat when he was promoted to orderly (first) sergeant on May 1. He replaced John Braden, who had been promoted to first lieutenant December 21, 1863. In that position Spawr was no longer in the color guard; he assisted officers by conveying orders, drilling the men, and so on (when he wasn't fighting).[112]

The Fourteenth Iowa was among part of Smith's command (under Brigadier General Joseph A. Mower) that was marched into the country to cover a large foraging party. The troops were attacked by Taylor's army and had to fight nearly every day for two weeks.[113] "The

112. Valentine L. Spawr army pension record; Thrift, *Roster and Record,* 758.

113. Burke, "From the 14th Iowa Infantry," July 1, 1864.

army is now protecting General Banks's army, whose principal business seems to be speculating in cotton and sugar," the entry in Shaw's brigade's itinerary for April 30 says. "Officers and men are heartily disgusted with this kind of service, and desire to be placed where they can act with honor to themselves and be of service to their country."

Scott was not happy about the brigade being ordered ten miles out on the Opelousas road south of Alexandria May 3 and forming a line of battle there.

> The ostensible purpose of occupying this position was the securing of forage; but as scarcely any was procured, and several thousand bushels of corn were carelessly burned, it was thought a somewhat suspicious circumstance that a large ginning establishment which was covered by our lines was turning out some fifteen or twenty bales of cotton per day. But, whether well founded or not, the impression was well nigh universal, that army movements were controlled to a considerable extent by the cotton interests. Such a state of affairs was most demoralizing and disheartening.

Burke described the conditions for the troops.

> The water we drank on these fatiguing marches was that which was obtained from bayous or sloughs, except occasionally a small quantity could be obtained from the cisterns near the plantation residences. The cisterns are built above the surface of the earth as the water keeps much cooler than when built under ground. The Red river looks quite red—hence the name, and is not wholesome to drink.
>
> . . . The weather was pretty hot from the 1st until the 10 of May, when there was some rain. The weather then turned suddenly cool, and, on the morning of the 12th of May there was a white frost plainly discernable in our camp near the city.

On the evening of May 13, they joined the rest of Smith's forces at Governor Thomas Moore's plantation. Lieutenant Colonel Joseph Bailey's dam had succeeded in raising the level of the Red River enough to allow the fleet to pass down it, and the retreat was resuming. Banks evacuated Alexandria May 14, and his army started moving south again. Smith's command marched out from the plantation that morning, covering the retreat of the army again.

One More Red River Battle

Captain Warren C. Jones, the Fourteenth Iowa's commander, was ill, and Captain Leroy A. Crane commanded the regiment on the march. They arrived at Marksville, near Fort DeRussy, the next evening. "On the night of the 15th of May the 14th Iowa went into camp where they had fought two months before," Burke wrote. Now they were giving up what they had won.

The fleet continued downstream from there, and the next morning the army began marching back to Simmesport on the route it had traveled up to Fort DeRussy in March. Taylor's army opposed the retreating army in front and harassed its flank and rear. "Skirmishing more or less severe occurred every day of the march until the 18th," the itinerary for Shaw's brigade says.[114]

The advance of the army reached Atchafalaya Bayou May 17 and threw a pontoon bridge (made by placing steamboats side by side) across the bayou, which was about a third of a mile wide. The detachments of the Sixteenth Corps, commanded by Mower, crossed Yellow Bayou and stopped four miles short of the Atchafalaya near

---

114. Donnan, William G. "A Reminiscence of the Last Battle of the Red River Expedition," *Annals of Iowa* 6 (1904), 241–247. https://doi.org/10.17077/0003-4827.2969

Yellow Bayou's intersection with Bayou des Glaises. They were to keep the rebels back while the wagon trains and main body of Banks's army passed.

On the morning of May 18, the Confederates appeared in force in the rear, and Mower ordered Shaw's and two other brigades with two batteries to cross back over Yellow Bayou and meet them. "A severe engagement ensued against numbers largely superior to our own, while the balance of our army lay quietly 3 miles distant from the action," Shaw's itinerary says. They drove the Confederates nearly two miles and found them in a belt of timber. The rebels opened fire with twelve pieces of rifled artillery, and Mower formed a battle line with two of the brigades. He left Shaw's brigade on the left and in the rear in reserve. The Fourteenth Iowa's part was to first march to a belt of timber and then "by left flank" into it to support the Ninth Indiana Battery. After they endured heavy artillery fire for a couple of hours, Shaw sensed an imminent attack on the left and ordered his brigade into an advanced line to the left of and nearly perpendicular to the line of battle formed by the other brigades. The Confederates charged out of the timber almost immediately. Their line was parallel to Shaw's new line, confirming his suspicion. Captured Confederate officers said after the battle that they were confident they had "turned" Mower's left flank and would capture all of his men. After the Fourteenth repulsed the Confederate charge there, it re-formed on the main line and again advanced under heavy fire. Mower had ordered the Union troops to charge with bayonets, and they repulsed the rebels "with terrible slaughter."[115]

Of total casualties of 267, 48 were in Shaw's brigade. In the Fourteenth Iowa, Company A's James Baldwin, a wagoner from Davenport, Iowa, was wounded in the forehead and died later that day in Yellow Bayou. Company C's Thomas L. Davidson of Bremer County, Iowa, was wounded along with twelve others in the regiment. "Owing to the intense heat and necessary rapidity of our movements, many of the men were entirely exhausted and had to be carried from the field," Major G. A. Eberhart, then commanding officer of the Thirty-Second Iowa, wrote in his report of the battle.[116]

Shaw made his opinion of Banks clear in a sarcastic letter to his hometown newspaper, the *Anamosa Eureka,* dated May 23.[117] His side had 2,700 infantry, 600 cavalry, and 14 pieces of

115. Donnan, "Reminiscence of Last Battle."

116. Thrift, 756, 761.

117. "Letter from Col. Shaw," published June 10, 1864.

artillery against an enemy force of 8,000 infantry, 7,000 cavalry, and 23 pieces of artillery, he wrote.

> You may think it strange that with an army of 30,000 men we should not have had more men engaged on our side, but the matter is easily explained. The balance of Smith's forces were guarding the different approaches to Simmesport while Banks' army, consisting of over 20,000 men, were rushing across the Atchafalaya, leaving their baggage-wagons and every thing behind for us to protect. I am candid when I say that I think I could capture his whole army with 500 men, so demoralized are they by his Union sentiments and policy.

Shaw's brigade lay in line of battle all day Thursday, May 19, and beginning at 2 a.m. of May 20 left camp, again crossed Yellow Bayou, marched to the Atchafalaya, crossed, and camped on the other side. The next day they marched to the mouth of the Red River and embarked on transports the morning after that with no further pursuit by Taylor's army. They arrived back in Vicksburg early in the morning of May 24 for the first time since leaving March 10.

End of the Red River Expedition

Banks's retreat—and the Fourteenth Iowa's association with his army—had come to an end. Major-General Edward Canby took command of the Trans-Mississippi Department, and Smith now reported to him.

Shaw wrote his letter to his hometown newspaper about the battle at Yellow Bayou the day he reached Vicksburg. A couple of letters to the editor protested his criticism of Banks, the letter writers feeling as if the criticism was intended for everyone in Banks's army. Shaw wrote a couple of responses excepting General Smith's forces and the Thirteenth Army Corps from his definition of "Banks's army"—and proceeded to criticize Banks further.[118]

When they arrived at Vicksburg, Burke wrote, "many of the soldiers were becoming quite destitute," and the command tried to requisition clothing. The quartermaster of the post did not have a full supply, but Western Sanitary agents had shirts and distributed them.

Brigadier General Smith summarizedhis corps' participation in the Red River Campaign.

---

118. *Davenport Daily Gazette,* July 21, 1864; August 8, 1864; *Anamosa Eureka,* August 12, 1864.

> I captured with my command 22 pieces of artillery, 1,757 prisoners, and Fort De Russy, with a strong casemated battery, which the gunboats would not have been able to pass. My loss was 153 killed, 849 wounded, and 133 missing; total 1,135; also 1 6 mule wagon. My entire command numbered originally 9,200.

First Lieutenant Burke summarized the expedition a little differently: "Since the 10th of March last, I have marched four hundred miles, been in five battles, forty days' continual skirmishing, and had no small amount of hard bedding and bad sleeping."

Before the battle of Pilot Knob, Missouri (on the right). *Harper's Pictorial History of the Civil War,* Alfred H. Guernsey and Henry W. Alden, 1866 and 1894.

CHAPTER 7
TUPELO AND PILOT KNOB: A MIRACLE IF WE EVER RETURNED

After returning from the Red River Expedition, the Fourteenth Iowa had a break from constant marching and fighting. Colonel James I. Gilbert, until then commander of the Twenty-Seventh Iowa, was now in command of the Second Brigade, Third Division, Sixteenth Corps. Colonel William T. Shaw would move up to command the Third Division that summer.[119]

The Fourteenth Iowa had some action in Arkansas on the way up the Mississippi in June and in the battles at Harrisburg and Town Creek, Mississippi, in July. For some of the companies of the regiment, the battles in Mississippi were their last ones before being mustered out in November. The others, including the replacement companies B and C, fought in the battle at Pilot Knob, Missouri, in September.

---

119. George Howard in *Report of Adjutant General, 1865,* 1179; Gilbert in R. Scott, "Operations in Louisiana and Trans-Mississippi," 980; Redfield Proctor, compiler, "Correspondence, Etc.," Part 5 in Series 1, Vol. 38 of *War of the Rebellion,* 318.

On June 4 the Sixteenth Army Corps headed up the Mississippi River from Vicksburg on steamers, the Fourteenth Iowa again on the *W. L. Ewing.*

Old River Lake, Arkansas

A few weeks earlier, Confederate General John S. Marmaduke had placed a cavalry and two batteries (about eight hundred men) under the command of General Colton Greene on the west side of the Mississippi in the area of Lake Chicot, Arkansas, to harass Union boats on the river. The Second and Third Brigades of Brigadier General Joseph A. Mower's First Division as well as some of the cavalry (estimated at three thousand men) disembarked at Sunnyside Landing on June 5 to take care of rebels.

They camped on the river bank overnight, and early the next morning the Third Brigade started marching west along the south side of the oxbow lake toward Lake Village in heavy rain. About halfway to the village (several miles), Mower encountered the rebels, who retreated to heavy timber on the other side of a bayou that led southward from the lake. Brigadier General A. J. Smith, commander of the Sixteenth, sent in a battery to support the infantry, and they managed to silence the rebels after an hour or so.

The Third Brigade was running out of ammunition, so Smith sent the Second (including the Fourteenth Iowa) to relieve them. Captain Warren C. Jones's report of the Fourteenth's part was succinct.[120]

> At 12 m. the regiment took position on the left of the Lake Village road, the right resting upon the left of the Thirty-second Iowa Volunteer Infantry and fronting Fish Bayou, upon the opposite bank of which the rebels were posted, their batteries upon our front and right. The enemy opened upon us with solid shot, doing no damage. Our line then advanced steadily through a dead briar thicket until within 20 feet of the bayou, when we opened our fire in volley by battalions. The enemy replied, their balls passing over our heads. We continued our fire until the enemy broke and fled, leaving us masters of the field.

120. Burke, "From the 14th Iowa Infantry," July 1, 1864; Joseph A. Mower, letter report June 15, 1864, in R. Scott, "Operations in Louisiana and Trans-Mississippi," 972; Encyclopedia of Arkansas, "Engagement at Old River Lake," https://encyclopediaofarkansas.net/entries/engagement-at-old-river-lake-1120/; Gilbert, letter report June 7, 1864, in R. Scott, 980; Warren C. Jones, letter report June 7, 1864, in R. Scott, 981–982. A note on page 972 of the reports of the engagement in R. Scott says, "Known also as engagement at Ditch Bayou, Fish Bayou, Grand Lake, and Lake Village."

> The depth of the water in the bayou prevented our charging their batteries. No casualties.

Mower's other regiments were not as lucky; the two brigades had forty-three men killed, seventy wounded, and seventy missing. Union records estimate the Confederates had a hundred casualties, but Greene reported only four killed and thirty-three wounded.[121]

Smith's troops continued to Lake Village, where they converted houses to hospitals. "Fences, chicken coops, out buildings, and everything that would burn was used for fires to warm, dry, and cook food for the thoroughly drenched men," according to Encyclopedia of Arkansas. They embarked again the next day and continued up the river, "bound now for Memphis where the command expects to be paid," Orville Burke wrote in one of his letters to the editor.[122]

Battle of Harrisburg (Tupelo), Mississippi

The Fourteenth Iowa did not see action again until mid-July, when Smith was sent to Harrisburg, or Tupelo, Mississippi, from LaGrange, Tennessee. (The town of Harrisburg

---

121. George A. Otis, "Engagements and Battles," CXI; Colton Greene, letter report June 9, 1864, in R. Scott, 985.

122. Encyclopedia of Arkansas, "Engagement at Old River Lake"; Burke, "From the 14th Iowa Infantry," July 1, 1864.

no longer exists; it was renamed Tupelo and incorporated after the Civil War. The official reports refer to Tupelo.) Smith's command had been charged with keeping the Confederates under Lieutenant General Stephen D. Lee and Major General Nathan B. Forrest from striking into middle Tennessee and destroying the railroad General William T. Sherman was using to get supplies in his Atlanta campaign. Smith reported that his object was "to secure Tupelo thus gaining possession of the railroad."[123]

Incidentally, the Third Division was commanded by Colonel David Moore on this expedition; Colonel William T. Shaw, who was the commander later in the month, was not mentioned in any of the reports.

The rebels attacked Smith's forces in Harrisburg several times and from different directions July 14, but they fell back under heavy fire each time. The Fourteenth Iowa, again commanded by Captain W. J. Campbell of Company K, did not participate in this fighting because it was assigned to guard the wagon train parked about two miles west of the town. However, one of its men was killed and several

123. American Battlefield Trust, "Civil War Overview: Tupelo," https://www.battlefields.org/learn/articles/tupelo; Andrew J. Smith, letter report August 5, 1864, in Stephen B. Elkins, 251.

wounded because they were in range of rebel guns.

Among the wounded from Company A were William Davenport of Davenport, Iowa (left ankle), Seventh Corporal Christian Litscher of Walnut Grove, Iowa (shoulder), George Turner of Davenport (thigh and arm), and First Corporal James M. Vanduzer of LeClaire, Iowa (right shoulder). (Vanduzer's injury was described as "severe," but he was promoted to fifth sergeant July 22 and stayed with the regiment until it was mustered out. Davenport, however, died of his ankle wound.) Company B's John Kerr of Franklin, Iowa, was severely wounded in the left leg.[124]

At dark they went into camp at the edge of a nearby swamp, but the rebels made another advance and the regiment was ordered out with the rest of the brigade to drive them off. One soldier of the Fourteenth was wounded then under "severe musketry fire."

---

124. Smith in Elkins, 251; Campbell in Appendix K, "Reports of Battles, Skirmishes, Etc., and Histories of Regiments," 1086–1087; William H. Thrift, 755–781; "Memphis Correspondence: (Correspondence of Davenport Gazette)," *Davenport (Iowa) Daily Gazette,* signed "J. D." Unless otherwise noted, the rest of the information on the section of Tupelo comes from Appendix K of *Report of the Adjutant General and Acting Quartermaster General of the State, January 11, 1864, to January 1, 1865.*

The next morning, July 15, they discovered they were almost out of food and ammunition. Smith had been ordered to take ten days' worth of supplies on the expedition, but the bread from the commissary depot was already spoiled when it was dispensed to them. He decided he had to begin a return to LaGrange that day. They marched north and crossed Old Town Creek, stopped there, and camped late that afternoon.

Suddenly the rebels made a rush forward, driving in the Union cavalry, and started shelling the camp and supply train from a hill about three-quarters of a mile from their camp. Gilbert's Second Brigade was sent out to deal with them. He had to attack with only two of his four regiments, the Fourteenth Iowa and Twenty-Seventh Iowa, because he barely had time to deploy those two before he received orders to move forward in line in double-quick.

Campbell described the action.

> The brigade was moved out and formed into line of battle in a swamp, and then advanced, wading Town creek, which was about two feet deep. After passing through the swamp and creek, we reached a cornfield, and there met the enemy. Our boys moved forward with a yell, which gave the rebels such a shock that their lines were at once broken and their men

> so terrified that their officers could not rally them to make a stand, although trying it several times. The rebels were driven off in about half an hour, and the field left in our possession. During this engagement many of my men, who were already much fatigued by the march of the day and the excessively hot sun, were overcome with heat and dropped out of ranks, the charge being over three-fourths of a mile in length and through a cornfield; but nearly all came up and joined their respective companies as soon as circumstances would permit. In this engagement the regiment lost 2 killed and 15 wounded.

The charge on the Confederates was "gallant and desperate," according to a letter to the *Davenport (Iowa) Daily Gazette.*[125] It said the troops "were immediately ordered into line of battle, to fix bayonets and charge the enemy's position, which they did at a double-quick, and to reach the enemy we had to ford three ponds of water, waist deep; but Iowa's brave sons never falter, when heroic valor is required."

For another description, here is an excerpt from Gilbert's report. (Moore's report, written a

125. Dated July 26, 1864, and signed "Veritos"; published August 8, 1864.

couple of weeks later, contains the same sentence nearly word for word.)[126]

> The line scaled the fence, waded a stream nearly waist deep in water and mud, through the thick brush and timber, waded the second stream as deep as the first, and on through the belt of timber to the edge of a large field of growing corn, when it came in full sight of the rebel line, which, with its battle-flags waving in the sunlight, was boldly and firmly advancing, pouring in a destructive fire.
>
> Gilbert ordered his line to fire and advance.
>
> The whole line poured in a volley, raised a shout, scaled the fence, and pressed steadily forward, firing as they advanced. The ground was rough and ascending, the day was very hot; by the time the line had reached the center of the field, many had dropped on the ground from heat and exhaustion.

But they were able to drive the rebels over the crest of the hill, and the firing stopped.

In Company A, Cornelius Fechter of Davenport was wounded in the left shoulder and Richard Fitzgerald of Walnut Grove, Iowa, was

126. Moore in Elkins, 281.

wounded in the left arm. Company B's Levi P. Hawley of Jacksonville, Iowa, was wounded in the right side. He had just been promoted to eighth corporal July 1.[127]

They resumed their trip back to LaGrange the next day. Smith left about forty of the men most severely wounded at Tupelo along with the Confederate injured that were left behind. "The line officers and soldiers deserve lasting praise for the manner in which they endured the hardships and fatigues of the campaign," Smith wrote in his report. "Marching over dusty roads with only one-half or one-third rations under a broiling sun with little water is certainly a severe test of their zeal and patriotism. All honor be to the noble men whose breasts are the bulwarks of our nation." The command ended their seventeen-day trip back at LaGrange on the morning of July 21.[128]

The wounded who were not left at Tupelo were taken to Memphis, arriving July 20. A correspondent who signed the initials J. D. wrote to the *Davenport (Iowa) Daily Gazette* that they

> had been conveyed from the field of action over rough roads, in army wagons, 85 miles, to Lagrange, where they took the cars [train]. The weather being intensely hot, and the

127. Thrift, 755–781.
128. Smith in Elkins, 252–253.

wounds of many being severe, nearly six days were occupied in reaching Lagrange. The wonder was that many did not die from the effects of the travel.

Among them was Davenport, who had received a flesh wound on his left ankle while guarding the wagon train at Tupelo. Eighteen years old when he enlisted in 1862, he was the grandson of the man for whom the city of Davenport was named and the son of a prominent Davenport businessman. "He was the picture of good health and spirits," J. D. wrote, and "said he would be all right in a few days." Then gangrene set in. "From that moment he was certain he must die, and also expressed himself as perfectly willing and even anxious to go." He declined rapidly and died August 6, 1864.[129]

Battle of Pilot Knob, Missouri

The Fourteenth Iowa camped at Memphis for a few weeks, made a mostly uneventful march to Oxford, Mississippi, and back, spent more time in camp at Memphis, and then moved to Cairo, Illinois, on its way to support General William T.

---

129. *Davenport (Iowa) Daily Gazette,* August 16, 1864. The letter written by "J. D." said he died August 5; Thrift's *Roster and Record,* 360, said it was August 6.

Sherman. However, Major General William S. Rosecrans urgently requested Major General H. W. Halleck to send Brigadier General A. J. Smith and the Sixteenth to St. Louis to help him protect the city from General Sterling Price's feared invasion of Missouri. Smith arrived at a camp near Jefferson Barracks, Missouri, September 15 with parts of two divisions numbering about 4,500 men.[130]

"No one appears to know what we are brought here for," Burke wrote in another letter to the editor of the *Anamosa (Iowa) Eureka* two days later.[131] What he does know is that he has a problem with Sanitary Commission agents.

> I know of my own knowledge and from good information and belief that much of what the good ladies of the Union donate for the sick and wounded soldier never reaches them—their object is good, but the Machinery by which the stores are conveyed is imperfect. It would be better to express *direct* to the soldier or some one of the company, or else in selecting Chaplains, Doctors or persons about hospitals for agents, to entrust those only with

130. Unless otherwise noted, the information in the Pilot Knob section, including the memories of the participants, is from Peterson and Hanson, *Pilot Knob.*

131. "From the 14th Iowa," published September 19, 1864.

the luxuries that are honest. It would be well for the Sanitary Societies of Iowa to look into this matter and ascertain if the clothes and nice provisions sent to the Soldiers Home in Memphis, Cairo and elsewhere on the River, are not too frequently used by Hospital pimps and women that do not deserve to be called *ladies.*

A Chance to Delay Price

When Price was ready to make his move into Missouri, he had three divisions which had among them eight brigades, several unattached regiments and battalions, four batteries, and one section of field artillery with fourteen pieces. He estimated he had 12,000 men, but only 8,000 were armed. (Other estimates of his forces vary widely.) The three divisions—commanded by Major General J. F. Fagan, Major General J. S. Marmaduke, and Brigadier General Joseph O. Shelby—traveled in separate columns to spread out foraging.[132]

Rosecrans didn't know what route Price would take as he came north from Arkansas. Besides protecting the city of St. Louis, Rosecrans also was concerned about the supply depots in

132. Peterson and Hanson, *Pilot Knob,* 36, 37 (citing Vol. 41 of *War of the Rebellion,* 627, 641), 80.

Springfield and Rolla (about a hundred miles southeast of St. Louis), the South Branch Railroad connecting Rolla and St. Louis, and the 900-wagon trains moving supplies from the end of the railroad at Rolla to Springfield. To keep Price from reaching the supplies and to delay him from reaching St. Louis, Rosecrans counted on a small, badly located fortification at Pilot Knob, eighty-six miles southeast of St. Louis.

Fort Davidson was just southwest of the village of Pilot Knob in the northern part of the Arcadia Valley. It had been built in the summer of 1863 of packed earth in a hexagon with each wall about 150 feet long, 9 feet high, and 10 feet thick. The only access across a dry moat surrounding it was one drawbridge at its southeast corner. It had two rifle pits extending from it. It lay between the north sides of Shepherd Mountain to the west and the knob (which gave the name to the town) to the east. Each hill rose abruptly to 500 to 600 feet, and each was covered with rocks, oaks, and undergrowth on the side facing the valley. Shepherd Mountain had several roads on the south and west sides leading to the summit.[133]

---

133. Missouri State Parks, "Historic Site History at Battle of Pilot Knob State Historic Site: The Battle of Pilot Knob," https://mostateparks.com/page/54963/historic-site-history; Mary Eakins Bullis, Missouri Civil War, "Fort Davidson, Battle of Pilot

When it was apparent Price was heading for Pilot Knob, the fort was occupied by a small garrison. Seven companies of the Forty-Seventh Missouri Infantry and the Fiftieth Missouri Infantry—all new troops—a company each of the First and Second Missouri Militia infantries, portions of companies of the Third Missouri Militia Cavalry, and a battery were under the command of Major James Wilson there. To reinforce Wilson's militia and untried volunteers, Rosecrans sent Brigadier General Thomas Ewing Jr., commander of the District of St. Louis, with Smith's Fourteenth Iowa, commanded by Captain William J. Campbell.

Ewing and the Fourteenth traveled to Mineral Point, Missouri, by the St. Louis and Iron Mountain Railroad September 25, leaving Companies A, G, H, I, and K at points along the rail line to strengthen garrisons guarding bridges. The next day, Companies B, C, D, and E and the colors continued on to Pilot Knob, where the rail line ended, and then marched two miles south from there to Ironton. The *Philadelphia Inquirer* and the *New York Times* estimated this detachment of the Fourteenth had about 130 men.[134]

Knob State Historic Site," http://missouricivilwar.net/fort-davidson/index.htm.

134. Campbell in letter report October 3, 1864, "Reports of Battles, Skirmishes, Etc., and Histories of Regiments," Appendix E in *Report*

With the Fourteenth Iowa detachment, "a company of colored men, collected and organized Monday afternoon preceding the assault," and "about thirty-five citizens who took arms and fought with us like veterans" added to the Missouri troops, they had 868 "effective men," according to Colonel Thomas Fletcher of the Forty-Seventh Missouri. Ewing put Fletcher in command of all the infantry forces.

Price Appears

By then Price, who had entered Missouri September 20, had reached Fredericktown, only twenty-one miles southeast of Pilot Knob. He sent Shelby's column north to destroy railroad track and bridges, leaving Fagan's and Marmaduke's divisions to attack Fort Davidson.

Campbell's official report says that after getting off the train at Pilot Knob on September 26 the Fourteenth "marched to Ironton, distant one mile [south of Pilot Knob], and camped for the night." They did more than that. Fagan's division entered Arcadia Valley below Ironton that afternoon, and the Fourteenth joined the

---

of the Adjutant General, 196; "A Gallant Little Campaign," *Philadelphia Inquirer,* October 11, 1864; "From Missouri," October 2, 1864, *New York Times.*

Missourians "on the double-quick and trot" to try to stop the Confederates.

Captain William V. Lucas of Company B remembered he'd gone into a barber shop when they reached town. The barber had shaved only half of his two-week beard when the long roll sounded and Lucas dashed out to lead his company. He said he endured many jokes until he was able to get the other half of his face shaved six days later. An Irishman in his company, Jimmy Boyle, told him, "Ah, bedad, what a foine lookin' corpse ye will make, so ye will."

Campbell's and Wilson's forces were able to drive the rebels back through the gap to the east of Ironton at dusk. "The effectiveness of the fire of the veterans of the 14th Iowa . . . was conspicuous wherever they were engaged," a Missouri cavalryman remembered forty years later. At the end of the day, however, the Union troops fell back to where they started in Ironton.

Wilson's and Campbell's orders were to spend the night with their men in line of battle about a mile below Ironton, so they set up camp behind an apple orchard. Soon the rebels reappeared and started setting up their own camps without seeing the Union troops. That was when Wilson and Campbell realized they were dealing with Price's whole army. Soon the lower portion of the valley was lit up by campfires. "We lay there in plain sight of all that was going on before us, but we dared not speak above a whisper lest we alarm the enemy. We could distinctly hear them boast how they would 'get away with that little fort' in the morning," Campbell wrote forty years later. After a couple of attempts, they got Ewing—who could not believe how many of the rebels were there at first—to let them retire to Ironton. Campbell first had his men rest near that town's courthouse, but when it began to rain, he moved them into the building "for shelter, but not to sleep."

"We gladly obeyed the order and spent the remainder of the night under shelter," Lucas wrote years later, "but we suffered from cold and hunger."

> These discomforts, however, were not so much thought of as what daylight would reveal to us. Every man realized that the position we were in was a perilous one if not absolutely hopeless. Before us was a large veteran army, determined to sweep the State with the besom [broom] of its power. To attempt to stand before it seemed sheer folly, to retreat from it was to court almost certain captivity or death. But the stake we were playing for was the rich city of St Louis, holding millions of dollars' worth of Government supplies, while its

capture would add great prestige to the Confederacy. General Ewing, after consulting with his officers, determined to delay the advancing enemy until reinforcements arrived. It was well we did not know then,—nor did we realize it until after the battle was fought,—that Smith's forces had been drawn back to the immediate vicinity of St. Louis for the more certain protection of the city, leaving us a forlorn hope to take care of ourselves as best we might.

The Battle

At daybreak the next morning, September 27, Campbell and his men heard shots as he was rousing them and rushing them into position. A Confederate cavalry was chasing the Union cavalry pickets into Ironton. Ewing's artillery opened fire on the rebels, and the battle was on. Wilson ordered Campbell to double-quick his men up an alley while he closed up the rear. When they had passed through the gap into the part of the valley where Pilot Knob lay, they stopped to form a line of battle. It was a cool morning with a drizzling rain. Campbell ordered rations for his men, and they were handed hardtack and raw bacon as they stood in line.

There they would have been in the line of fire from the fort's artillery, so Campbell got permission to move onto a spur of Shepherd Mountain. That required marching through timber to the crest of a ridge. Some of the Confederates followed them, but the Fourteenth's rapid fire kept them from overtaking them. Then another rebel brigade went around the hill to the west and approached their rear. The Fourteenth had to turn to fight in that direction. "The enemy was well protected by the trees, rocks, and brush; and as our line advanced upon them," Lucas wrote, "it was necessarily broken but it never wavered for a moment." Two men of Company E were killed.

Campbell described the escape of everyone else.

> We marched parallel with the valley until we struck a timber road. The underbrush was so thick and so difficult to penetrate that I took this old blind road, first sending two men ahead as scouts to watch for the enemy. They soon returned, reporting they heard voices in the brush that skirted the valley. I gave the command to file left, and struck into the brush and boulders. The hillside was steep and covered with loose rocks and undergrowth; this made marching difficult. After moving some two hundred yards further in this

> direction I determined to debouch into the valley. As we struck the open ground I gave the command, "Head of column to the left; double-quick march!"

They moved between the two bodies of the Confederates that had been closing in on them, crossed the crest, and entered the fort's south rifle pit.

In the meantime, Wilson had taken a similar position on Pilot Knob and was captured.

After the Fourteenth was off Shepherd Mountain, the Confederates dragged two field guns to the summit and leveled a spot for them. As soon as they fired their first shot at the fort, the artillery there shot back and disabled the Confederate gun. The rebels had to move back farther from the fort.

The guns of the fort stopped the Confederate advance up the center of the valley for a time. By midday, however, Marmaduke's division had arrived and the Confederates lined up across the plain south of the fort. Their line of battle extended up the sides of Shepherd Mountain and Pilot Knob.

Ewing directed Campbell to leave the fort again and take the Fourteenth back to Shepherd Mountain. This time he wanted them on the north end (just south of the fort). "I passed out of the fort, knowing that to obey meant capture or a miracle if we ever returned," Campbell wrote years later. Once there, he deployed Company D as skirmishers and sent reconnaissance reports back to Ewing.

At about two o'clock, according to Private Azariah Martin of the Forty-Seventh Missouri Volunteer Infantry, "a fearful volley was poured into the Fourteenth Iowa boys on Shepherd's Mountain from the ravine on the northeastern side of the mountain."

> Two of the boys of the 14th were wounded and fell down the steep mountain side but with the coolness of veterans the remainder of the detachment descended from their position, carefully picked up their two wounded comrades, and supported them into the fort, passing us as they went in. Immediately after[,] I saw the whole side of Shepherd's Mountain become fairly black with the mass of the enemy who came rushing down upon the flat toward us.

A correspondent for the *St. Louis Democrat* called the Fourteenth Iowa "a regiment that covered itself all over with glory."[135]

135. "Latest from Pilot Knob—Gallantry of Gen. Ewing—A Carnival of Blood—Horrible Butcheries at Potosi, &c.,"

Twice the Confederates demanded Ewing surrender. After consulting all the officers, he said, "They will play no Fort Pillow game on me" and sent word back that he would fire on the next flag of truce the Confederates sent forward. The Confederates attacked.

The Fourteenth "was compelled to fall back within the fort when a general engagement commenced," Campbell wrote in another understatement in his 1864 report. Ewing and the Missouri forces within the fort waited for the rebels to charge and then "opened with shell, grape, cannister and musketry." The rebels fell back, but then they started moving up the sides of the surrounding mountains to attack from there.[136]

Soon all the Union forces were inside the fort or its rifle pits firing at the rebels surrounding them. Sergeant H. C. Wilkinson of the Forty-Seventh Missouri described the scene inside when he went in from the south rifle pit.

Philadelphia Inquirer, October 6, 1864, from *St. Louis Democrat,* October 3, 1864.

136. Campbell, "Reports of Battles, Skirmishes, Etc., and Histories of Regiments," Appendix E in *Report of the Adjutant General,* 197; "Details of the Invasion," *New York Times,* October 5, 1864; "From Missouri," *New York Times,* October 10, 1864.

I saw the stately form of General Ewing, his arms folded, his mouth tightly closed, and his face slightly pale, but firm as a "stone wall." He was walking erect from side to side, looking here and there at the surging mass around us. Then came the wounded lieutenant of the brave old Fourteenth Iowa (Lieut. Smith Thompson) limping hither and thither, cheering the boys to do their best. I could see Captain Campbell, Adjutant Murphy, and other gallant officers, rushing from side to side and using all the power that was in them to direct and encourage the boys who were then down on their knees at the parapets, pouring lead into those charging hosts of the enemy. Oh, but it was hot there! In a moment our smoke hung like a dense cloud about two feet above the parapet, while the smoke from the enemy's muskets came down almost to their knees, hiding their bodies, though beneath the smoke we could see the swarms of fast moving legs and feet as they seemed to swerve about from left to right, from right to left. Lieutenant Settle afterward told me that from his position on Shepherd's Mountain Fort Davidson looked like a mighty, burning tar-kiln as our smoke rose slowly heavenward.

Sergeant James C. Steakley of Company K of the Third Missouri State Militia Cavalry also described the scene.

> Inside, in the center of the fort, was the magazine with the flag-pole on top of it and Old Glory floating at its peak as beautiful as ever except that the drizzling rain prevented it from swinging out as buoyantly as the heart would wish on such an occasion. . . . The men with small arms stood four to six deep around the inside of the walls, especially on the side next the enemy.
>
> . . . So far as I could see every man in the fort was all enthusiasm and fight, each vieing with the comrade next him to shoot the fastest and most accurately.

"The battle had now reached its height of fury and carnage," Campbell wrote years later. "The enemy's ranks were being decimated by our musketry while our artillery tore great gaps through them." Many of the accounts written by veterans of the battle praised Colonel David Murphy, who was commanding the artillery.

"I do not recall a single shot falling into the fort during the afternoon; the damage was all done by their sharpshooters picking off our gunners," Sergeant Major John H. Delano of the

Forty-Seventh Missouri Infantry Volunteers wrote later.

The Confederates were forced back but re-formed and made a second charge. "Again they broke in confusion, our fire still dealing death and destruction through their ranks," Campbell wrote. The Confederates then made a third charge, "and only veteran soldiers can appreciate what that means. If this could be repulsed, the worst part of the battle would be over." The approaching rebels were in three long lines, each four ranks deep, coming from two directions. The troops in the fort mowed them down with artillery and muskets. When the rebels reached the ditch and started down into it, the men in the fort started throwing hand grenades into it.

> Pandemonium instantly broke loose. Above the roar of the battle it was a perfect saturnalia of the damned. Men were blown above the parapet and fell back dead; the ditches were cleared as if by magic. It struck terror to the enemy's lines and they fell back in disorder; but our fire never slackened until they were out of range. It was now sundown and night closed the contest.

According to Campbell, Ewing announced after the battle that his battalion of the Fourteenth had saved the fort. He put Campbell in charge of the works, the post sentries, lowering away the gate, assisting the surgeons and their attendants in caring for the wounded, and allowing or not allowing anyone to pass in or out.

Fletcher described the scene outside the fort after the Confederates left.

> When the final desperate charge had been fully repulsed, the last ray of the setting sun had faded from the mountain top and the evening shadows were beginning to fall in the valley. The firing ceased; not a shot was heard; the silence was broken only by the groans of the wounded who lay everywhere on the field. The enemy was scattered in the gullies, ravines, and behind logs,—in every place of concealment,—waiting the coming of darkness to cover their retreat. . . . We proceeded to care as best we could for the wounded; both our own and the Confederates who were left on the field near the fort. The dead were left where they fell. The Confederate killed and wounded, as the count was subsequently given to me by persons who made it, numbered 1,468, and long after the battle a number of bodies that had not been included in the count, were found on the mountain sides.

Union officers later estimated the Confederate killed and wounded (and left on the field) at 1,500 to 2,000. Ewing's losses for his entire operation were estimated at 150. Among them was Charles I. Thorp of Company B. (Unlike any other death in the roster, the Iowa adjutant general's roster and record describes his death as "died of gunshot wounds" rather than "killed in action.") John R. Cummins of Company C was wounded and died of his wounds a month later in Cape Girardeau, Missouri. Eighteen-year-old William Mowfield, one of the Columbus enlistees, was taken prisoner.[137]

"A fearful task was before us," Wilkinson wrote.

> Two-thirds of the circumference of the fort,—east, south, and west,—were surrounded by a dense mass of infantry, their guns were still hurling shot and shell at the fort from the heights beyond, and out of the west and northwest came Slayback and Freeman with a dark cloud of cavalry to cut us down if we attempted to escape.

137. "Details of the Invasion"; "From Missouri"; Thrift, 760, 771, 777.

One of the wounded Confederate officers had told a surgeon that evening that the rebels were building ladders to attack the fort at daylight.

Ewing met with his officers to decide whether to stay and fight the next day or to try to evacuate. Fletcher summarized the dilemma.

> Here we were, completely surrounded with an overwhelming force, without hope of re-enforcement or succor. It was plain that we could not stay there and very nearly as plain that we could not get away. Our only course was conceded to that we must make the effort to escape and take the chances.

Perhaps still bitter about the way the battle of Pleasant Hill ended, Campbell was one of the ones who argued in favor of staying and fighting. He was ready to fight the Confederates the next day with only the detachment of the Fourteenth. However, the officers held a secret ballot and evacuation won by one vote. Preparations began at midnight.

Ewing described the way their plans unfolded.[138]

> The works of the Iron Company, at the north base of Pilot Knob had been fired by the

138. Thomas Ewing in Vol. 11, *Rebellion Record,* 137.

> enemy, and the immense pile of charcoal glowed and flamed all night, making the valley as light as noonday. . . . I had Colonel Fletcher arrange for having the magazine (which was large and filled with every variety of ammunition) blown up two hours after we left, or as soon as our exit should be discovered by the enemy. . . . The garrison was then aroused, knapsacks packed, haversacks and cartridge boxes well supplied, and everything destructible, which we could not take away and the enemy might use, placed near or on the magazine. At three o clock Colonel Fletcher silently led the infantry out of the sally-port, around the ditch and through the north rifle pit, forming them under the cover of a deep shadow at the end of the pit. The drawbridge was then covered with tents to muffle the sound, and the cavalry and battery, marching out, formed column with the infantry, and took a by-way to the Potosi road. We left Slayback's camp on our right, and another rebel camp near the road on our left, both unapprised of our movement. The body of the rebel army was at Ironton.

Bodies of some of the fallen Union men were left near the pile that was to be blown up.

Years later, Sergeant Major Lewis Sutton of the Fourteenth Iowa described the regiment's role in the evacuation. His and Campbell's versions are the only ones that say that Campbell was present at the officers' meeting and that the Fourteenth was in the advance when they left.

> The men were told to take what hardtack they could, while Captain Campbell saw that each man had a hundred rounds of ammunition. The artillerymen made ready their guns on muffled wheels and the arrangements were complete. General Ewing assigned to the Fourteenth Iowa the first position in the column and the honor of leading the way. Captain Campbell gave strict orders to keep in ranks and well did his men understand the situation.

Ewing ordered Campbell to take up a line of march northward on the Caledonia road, and a number of civilian refugees fell in with the troops. When the Confederates heard the blast of the magazine blowing up, they assumed it was accidental and were not concerned about it. They did not discover the fort was empty until about eight Wednesday morning. When they did, Marmaduke's division headed after the escapees.

Ewing started to head north to Mineral Point, but when they entered Caledonia at about sunrise his men captured a member of an advance guard of Shelby's cavalry. They learned from him that the Union troops there had fallen back and Shelby had taken nearby Potosi. Ewing immediately changed his route to march to the northwest. Shelby waited for them above Caledonia for several hours before he discovered they had left the road; that gave them a head start, which they needed because the cavalry could travel faster than the infantry. They marched thirty miles that day and camped at Webster at sunset with coffee, hardtack, and bacon, the first food they had had for 30 hours.[139]

A Dark, Wet March on a Few Hours' Sleep

At one a.m. on Thursday, September 29, the troops resumed the march with the Fourteenth Iowa in the rear. During their rest, Ewing had decided to travel to Harrison (now known as Leasburg) because the road there traveled along a spur of the Ozark range and would be easier to defend than the route to Rolla.[140]

---

139. Ewing, 138; Campbell in "Reports of Battles, Skirmishes, Etc., and Histories of Regiments," Appendix E in *Report of the Adjutant General,* 197.

140. Ewing, 138.

All of the accounts of that night mention how dark and wet it was. Lucas provided details.

> When we were on our road again, to add to our hardships rain began to fall, and it continued to fall all night in torrents. It was inky dark and the road crossed the crooked little river every half-mile or so. We blundered along over stumps and stones and against trees, plunging into the stream, which was rapidly rising from the heavy downpour, and the waters of which were often so deep as to strike the shorter men about their armpits. We caught one another's hands so that if a man fell or was swept off his feet, he would not be lost.

Some of the men held their guns reversed with the locks under their armpits to keep the priming dry.

Sutton also described what the march was like for the Fourteenth.

> General Ewing now assigned the Fourteenth Iowa to the rear, that being the important position. As we started there was sharp lightning and rain and the thunder was very heavy and seemed low and close, as if to awaken the tired sleepy soldiers and hurry them on their way. The night was so intensely dark that the men could not see one another

> and the trees beside the road formed almost an arch of black foliage overhead. A little creek (the Courtois), swollen by the rain until it was nearly two feet deep and from fifteen to twenty feet wide, had to be waded six or eight times. The road could only be found by the aid of a lantern carried in front; and a few candles, which had been procured at Webster, were cut in short pieces, lighted, and placed by the side of the road. When the candles were gone, a bugle was sounded in front, but the night was too dark for the column to follow such a leader; and finally a halt was ordered to wait for daylight.

They had been able to travel only eight miles.

The regiment was called into action first thing in the morning, according to Ewing.[141]

> We had just reached the ridge at eight o clock Thursday morning when the enemy charged upon our rear guard and drove it upon the column. I placed the detachment of the Fourteenth Iowa infantry,—Co, H, Forty-seventh Missouri, Co's C, D, and K, Third Missouri State Militia Cavalry,—and Lieutenant Smiley's section of artillery, in the rear, all under command of Major Williams, Tenth

141. Ewing, 138.

> Kansas, acting aide-de-camp, and, with occasional halts to rake the woods with shell and canister, we made a good and successful march, the enemy almost constantly engaged with our rear guard but unable to break through or flank it.

"I especially remembered the men of a detachment of an Iowa regiment who proved themselves all heroes," Captain H. B. Milks of the Third Missouri State Militia Cavalry wrote years later.

The Fourteenth Fights for the Last Time

"Our halts, though frequent, were brief," Ewing wrote, "and were only to unlimber the artillery, stagger the pursuers with a few rounds, and move on." When they came within four miles of Harrison, Ewing wrote, "There the road debouches on a high sweep of gently rolling woodland and from that we fought hard for every step we gained."

The Confederates caught up with them again when they were about a mile from the town. They tried to stampede the escapees, and it almost worked. Ewing complained that the panicking of "the refugees,—men, women, and children, white and black" who were traveling with them nearly sacrificed the command.

A Missouri battery stopped and formed facing east with Missouri infantry and cavalry on its left and the Fourteenth Iowa on the right. (The road approached Harrison/Leasburg from the south-east.) "Some of the organized companies of infantry were very much excited with the fear of being taken and killed," wrote Missouri cavalry-man Steakley, "and chances seemed so much against us that even some of the mounted men who had seen three years of service and who I thought would never flinch became frightened and ran away."

The Fourteenth Iowa veterans, however, impressed Steakley. "In the midst of all this confusion and alarm," he wrote, "I heard the command, 'Fall in here, Fourteenth Iowa. D—n them, we can whip them ourselves!'"

> How encouraging it was to see that veteran captain, with his sword in his right hand and his hat in his left, forming his men steadily under the muzzles of the right wing of Battery H, and to hear him call out,
>
> "Right dress! Front! Forward, march! Double-quick, march!"
>
> Then forward they went, like Spartans of old; and when about one hundred and fifty or two hundred yards in front of the battery they

> halted, dressed, and we could distinctly hear the officer call out:
>
> "Load! In nine times, load! Ready! Aim! Fire! Load! In nine times, load!" So simultaneous was their fire, that it sounded like the report of one gun, though as loud as a cannon. After about two hundred shots had been fired by Battery H, and probably twenty volleys by that brave little band of the Fourteenth Iowa, everything quieted down in the valley in front of us as if the enemy had seated themselves to take their after dinner smoke; and the guns limbered up and we went into column and jogged on into Leasburg without further trouble.

The Fourteenth did have some casualties, however, Sutton reported.

> Captain Campbell marched his troops across the field in line of battle, and when the woods were reached he filed into the road, while the enemy's bullets whistled through the trees. Here Lieut. John C. Braden of Co. C, Fourteenth Iowa, and our color sergeant and his guard, were wounded. When within a mile of Leasburg the Fourteenth Iowa was formed in line of battle in rear of the command and

marched thus to the station, with the Confederates close behind.

Braden died of his wounds in Rolla a month later. The Fourteenth's color bearer, Second Corporal Edwin H. Tyler of Company B, also was severely wounded in the fight. John Nergo of Company B was taken prisoner at some point during the march.[142]

Typically, Campbell described the preceding action in one sentence in the report he prepared at the time: "Arriving at Leesburg at sunset, my command formed in line of battle on the left, facing the enemy, where we remained encamped during the night."[143]

Surrounded and Cut Off

Infantry, cavalry, artillery, and civilians had traveled sixty-six miles through rough country in thirty-nine hours, or an average of a little more than one and two-thirds miles an hour, or forty and a half miles a day. They had not eaten since the night before except for a few turnips some of the Missourians broke out of line to gather as they marched.

142. Thrift, 758, 771.

143. Campbell, 197.

A freight train arrived in Harrison soon after they settled in, and at first the men thought they would be able to return to St. Louis on it. However, the Confederates quickly tore up the tracks on each side of the town. Ewing's men were now surrounded and cut off. One good thing was that the train was loaded with supplies—ammunition, hardtack, bacon, overcoats, blankets, picks, shovels, and so on.

Ewing had the men begin building temporary fortifications of railroad ties, cars, and other materials found around the depot, and the work on them continued the next day. That night he had the idea of setting a barn on fire to light up the open area south of the town so the rebels couldn't attack in darkness. Campbell asked Lucas for a "discreet and daring" volunteer, and Corporal Earl J. Lamson, who was nineteen when he enlisted in 1862, came forward. Lamson's wife and child happened to be living with Lucas's family back home in Iowa. Lamson said he was willing to risk the dangers and gave Lucas directions for the care of his family if he didn't return. He did return, the burning barn lit up the area overnight, and the rebels did not attack.

The rebels attacked a couple of times during the day, but Ewing chased them off by firing shells at them. He didn't know it at the time, but Shelby and Marmaduke had decided capturing them was no longer worth it and moved on, leaving just a few troops there. On Friday night Ewing sent a "citizen messenger" to Rolla with a couple of officers to plead for reinforcements. Finally, on the afternoon of October 2, a lookout with field glasses on the roof of the Lea hotel spotted riders approaching from the north. At first the barricaded troops thought it was more rebels, but it turned out to be the Seventeenth Illinois Cavalry, about six hundred men. The unnamed citizen messenger had succeeded.[144]

Stars and Stripes to the Rescue

Lucas described the emotions of the men when they saw their rescuers.

> The lookout electrified us by exclaiming:
>
> "They carry the stars and stripes!"
>
> Up to that moment I had never realized fully what the presence of the flag of my country meant. The tired, worn, powder-begrimed and dirt-stained men in the little fort cheered, clasped one another in their arms, shook hands, cried, leaped about, and generally acted like crazy men. In the midst of their rejoicing, I began to sing, "Yes, we'll rally round the flag, boys, we'll rally once again."

144. "From Missouri"; Ewing, 138.

> The refrain was caught up, and the welkin rang as we sang "with the spirit and the understanding." It was a joyful time, never to be forgotten by the participants.

At two a.m. the next day, October 3, Ewing's forces took up the line of march again and reached St. James on the South Pacific Railroad after traveling thirty miles. They were able to board the "cars" there and reached Rolla at six p.m.[145]

Lucas, who had spent the past six days with only one side of his face shaved, was finally able to have a barber finish the job. "While working the dirt and sand out of the 'long side,'" Lucas wrote, "the fellow's curiosity was excited until he could not refrain longer from comments. 'I nevah see a face befo', sah,' said he, 'dat one side was richer dan de odder; but yo's is, suah!' I then explained to him which seemed to afford him great relief."

"When the detachment reached Rolla," one historian wrote, "the men had been fighting, fighting and marching, for four days almost constantly."[146]

145. Campbell, 197; "From Missouri."

146. Ingersoll, *Iowa and the Rebellion,* 205–206.

> They had not had more than one hour's rest out of twenty-four, their feet were covered with blisters, but they had done their duty under a general who had done his and they marched into Rolla with feelings of pride quite unlike their feelings when they returned to Alexandria four months before.

Ewing and his assorted forces had not only escaped death or capture at Pilot Knob but had also succeeded in delaying Price for two days by fighting him in Arcadia Valley and for four more days by diverting Marmaduke's and Shelby's divisions during the retreat to Leasburg. Price's third division, Fagan's, could not have attacked St. Louis alone. Instead of moving east to St. Louis as he had planned, Price now headed north toward Jefferson City, the state capitol. By the time he arrived there, however, Union forces had been able to prepare for him. Price put on a show of attacking the city with his artillery but moved past it.

"General Price's failure at Jefferson City must be ascribed more or less directly to his delay at Pilot Knob and the results of the battle there," Cyrus Peterson and Joseph Hanson wrote in *Pilot Knob: Thermopylae of the West.*

> Had he not suffered that disastrous repulse, his officers and men would not have been so fearful of attempting the intrenchments of Jefferson City and might have succeeded in storming them. Furthermore, had he not wasted precious days in his operations against Pilot Knob and in a futile pursuit of Ewing's column, there can be little doubt that, even if he had abandoned his attack on St Louis, he could have reached Jefferson City before its earthworks would have been in condition to withstand an assault and before more than a handful of troops could have been concentrated for its defense.

He eventually returned to Arkansas at the end of the year without achieving his objective of occupying the state.

Meanwhile, the survivors of the battle of Pilot Knob and the march to Leasburg, Lucas wrote years later, had finally reached a "haven of rest and safety." The Fourteenth would not be sent out to fight for the Union again.

Colonel William T. Shaw, *History of Jones County, Iowa,* Volume 2, Robert McClain Corbit, S. J. Clarke Publishing Company, 1910.

CHAPTER 8
HAVING TO FIGHT FOR WHAT WAS RIGHT

Orville Burke wrote another letter to the *Anamosa (Iowa) Eureka* from Franklin, Missouri, October 6 ("From the 14th Infantry," published October 28, 1864).[147] He said the entire regiment had returned to Jefferson Barracks south of St. Louis and had then moved to Franklin. The men had no idea that their regiment's founder, commander, and hero was under attack from the army itself.

Colonel William T. Shaw: A Blunt Soldier and Honest Man

The first name listed in a column of dismissals for the week ending October 8, 1864, in *The Army and Navy Official Gazette* was one that few would expect: Colonel William T. Shaw, 14th Iowa Volunteers. He had been stripped of his command

147. Burke was not in the detachment that went all the way to Pilot Hill, and his letter is full of errors about the battle and the escape Ewing led; he does say, "The railroad and telegraph being destroyed in several places between here and Rolla, it is impossible, at present, to . . . get a correct and full account."

of the Third Division, Sixteenth Corps and dismissed from the Army October 4 "for violation of Army Regulations and General Orders from the War Department in regard to publications over his own signature in relation to operations of the armies of the United States in the Department of the Gulf."[148]

What publications? The dismissal could refer to any, all, or none of the following:

- *The undated letter (or "statement") quoted in at least three books in 1865 and 1866.* The author has not been able to find the complete letter or any record of its original publication in a newspaper or anywhere else.[149]

---

148. *Army & Navy Official Gazette,* Volume 2, 1864–1865, Washington City, 1865, 239.

149. The first, Stuart's *Iowa Colonels and Regiments,* published in 1865, 277–278, quoted just one paragraph and said it was an extract of what was published in the *Dubuque (Iowa) Times*. Colonel John Scott quoted more paragraphs—separated with asterisks—as part of his "History of the 32d Iowa" in *Report of the Adjutant General,* Appendix K, 326–327. Scott does not say it was published in a newspaper, and the compiler indexed it as a "statement." The author has not been able to find issues of the *Dubuque Times* for April–June 1864. Ingersoll, however, in *Iowa and the Rebellion,* 207–208, included extracts identical to the ones Scott used and says they were from a letter to a friend published in the *Anamosa Eureka.* The author has searched the *Anamosa Eureka* for April–June 1864 for the letter without finding it.

- *The letter the rebels captured with the mail after the battle of Pleasant Hill.* Was this letter the same as the previous letter?[150]
- *Shaw's official report, in letter format, of the Battle of Pleasant Hill published in the* Anamosa Eureka *June 24 that hinted at General William Dwight's drunkenness and was accompanied by an editor's note that Generals McMillan, Emory, and Dwight were so drunk they couldn't ride their horses.*[151]
- *The letter to the* Eureka *that Shaw wrote about Bayou des Glaises and defended a couple of times afterward.* These publications criticized General Nathaniel Banks's leadership, but they did not even hint at drunkenness.[152]

A statement about Shaw's dismissal ("Not Gen. Banks") in the *Davenport (Iowa) Daily Gazette* October 29, 1864, is not at all helpful. It says that the *Muscatine (Iowa) Journal* had misinterpreted "the *Gazette* statement" in saying that Shaw was dismissed for saying in the *Eureka* that Banks was drunk when he should have been leading his men in battle. To correct this, the *Daily Gazette* says, "The officer of whom

150. "Misrepresentations of Iowa Regiments."

151. "Battle of Pleasant Hill: Official Report of Col. Wm. T. Shaw."

152. "Letter from Col. Shaw," published June 10, 1864; "The Red River Expedition: Letter from Col. Shaw."

Col. Shaw wrote, and whose name we did not mention, was Gen. Emory." This probably refers to Shaw's official report, published in the *Eureka* June 24, but all that did was hint that Dwight (not Emory) was drunk. (The *Eureka* editor said both Dwight and Emory were drunk.)

The *Eureka* published an opinion and reprinted a couple of other Iowa newspaper opinions on the subject November 4. They all refer vaguely to a letter published in June. It appears not even the *Eureka* ("Col. Shaw") knows whether Shaw was punished for his letters to editors or for the official report. "His contempt and indignation found vent—and in direct contravention of a regulation of the War Department—through his letters to editors at home," the *Eureka* wrote. "In his report to the commanding General Col. Shaw did not spare these cowardly officers and so the facts go into official history."

The reprinted opinion of the *Davenport Daily Gazette* ("A Brave Iowa Officer Disgraced," same issue) quoted the dismissal order and opined, "In other words, Colonel Shaw wrote a letter to his home in Anamosa, published in the *Eureka* of that place, in which like a blunt soldier and honest man he told the truth of a certain General of the 16th Army Corps, who was beastly drunk when he ought to have been leading his men to the field." This, too, could have referred to the official report.

The opinion of the *Dubuque (Iowa) Times* ("A Reward for Bravery and Efficiency"), reprinted in the *Eureka* the same date, adds to the mystery. "Our readers will remember the scathing review of Gen. Banks's Red River expedition, published in these columns last June under Colonel Shaw's signature. We thought at the time that such a publication was indiscreet, and would injure the officer." He was being punished, it said, for "publishing facts in regard to the drunkenness and inefficiency of certain Generals." Was the *Times* lumping the official report and the Eureka editor's comment together the way the other newspapers seemed to do, or did that newspaper actually publish the mystery letter quoted in the books later? The author has not been able to locate the relevant issue of the *Dubuque Times* to see exactly what it published in June 1864.

An 1888 review of the controversy said Shaw was dismissed because of a letter to "a public journal" in which he accused several of Banks's officers of being drunken and incompetent at Pleasant Hill, which could mean either his official report or the mystery letter quoted in books in 1866. The account continues that "not less than twenty-five of Banks's officers as well as Banks himself . . . charged Shaw with incompetency, with fear, with cowardice, with ordering his men to run while terror had seized upon himself." The author commented, "It was not an uncommon belief that Shaw's peremptory dismissal without a trial was to preclude the possibility of his proving the truth of the charges he had made in the newspapers." The Secretary of War did not even give Shaw a hearing.[153]

General A. J. Smith refused to promulgate the order of dismissal, and it was never executed. The dismissal was revoked December 23, 1865, and Shaw was given an honorable discharge effective the same date the rest of his regiment was mustered out.[154]

When Shaw left the Third Division of the Sixteenth Army Corps, which he commanded the last few months of his service, the officers surprised him with a sword and scabbard from Tiffany as a memento of their respect. The sword was made of Damascus steel and had a hilt of solid silver mounted with gold. The scabbard also was solid silver and was triple plated and mounted with solid gold. The officers had raised $650 to have it made for him.[155]

---

153. Byers, 282–283.

154. Ingersoll, 209; Byers, 283.

155. "Testimonial to Col. Shaw," *Anamosa Eureka,* November 4, 1864.

Recruits for Old Regiments Will Be Discharged at the Original Time

The Fourteenth returned to Iowa on November 5, arriving at Davenport and entering Camp Kinsman. The replacement companies now had a new battle to fight. The three-year terms of the original Fourteenth Iowa regiment volunteers ended that fall, and the men in the three replacement companies had been promised they would be mustered out at the same time even though they had started service a year later.

Although Spawr's army file shows he enlisted for three years, orders from Iowa's adjutant general published in the Davenport *Daily Democrat & News* November 26, 1862, said he and others in the same situation wouldn't be held to that. The order quoted a letter from Brigadier General C. P. Buckingham of the War Department dated September 26, 1862, less than a month before Spawr enlisted. It said, "Recruits for old regiments of volunteers for three years or the war, will be discharged at the expiration of the time for which the regiment was originally enlisted." The adjutant general had published a circular in January 1864 again including the letter about the discharges.

In spite of recruiters' promises, reassurances from officials, and published official policy, however, the army in 1864 was requiring replacement recruits to serve for three full years beginning with their own enlistments rather than "at the expiration of the time for which the regiment was originally enlisted." In some instances officials began to say the replacement recruits would need to provide proof their recruiting officers promised them they would be discharged at the same time as of the original recruits.[156]

The *Daily Davenport Democrat* published the following opinion about the three replacement companies of the Fourteenth Iowa on November 10, 1864:

> The 14th Regiment—There is no doubt but a portion of this regiment—seven companies will be mustered out soon, but there are very serious doubts whether the companies that have served less than three years will be accorded that privilege. Regardless of promises made to recruits for old regiments, that they should be mustered out [at] the expiration of the regiment's term of service, the War Department has persistently refused to

156. "Information Wanted," signed by "War Widow," *Daily Davenport Democrat,* June 29, 1864; "Remonstrance of Iowa Soldiers: They Ask for Justice," *Daily Davenport Democrat,* October 28, 1864.

> do so in a single instance—not a recruit from the Second Regiment up to the 14th has been mustered out as agreed upon, and it is hardly fair to presume that privileges that have been denied to recruits in every senior regiment will be accorded to recruits of the 14th. Though here in camp they have no right to expect any such partiality, and we predict that nothing of the sort will be done. It is true their enlistment was based on the promise of the War Department that their service should expire with the end of the three years for which the 14th was originally mustered, so it was with the recruits for the 2d Infantry, and they have not been mustered out yet, and probably will not be until they have served three years.

Two days later the *Daily Davenport Democrat* published a note ("Another Effort") saying Iowa Adjutant General N. B. Baker was trying again to let the replacement volunteers muster out with the rest of their regiments. Two days after that, on November 16, all of the Fourteenth Iowa was mustered out with no explanation reported in the news.[157]

The Fourteenth was the only Iowa regiment from the Second to the Seventeenth that did not

157. Thrift, *Roster and Record,* 731–879.

have enough soldiers re-enlist to keep its name and organization. "The reasons why the regiment refused to renew their enlistment need not be stated, for they involve an old feud, which should not be revived," Addison A. Stuart wrote in *Iowa Colonels and Regiments: Being a History of Iowa Regiments in the War of the Rebellion; and Containing a Description of the Battles in which They Have Fought.* Presumably he refers to Shaw's dismissal.[158]

Compare the Fourteenth's return to Iowa with its departure the previous year, again described in the *Daily Davenport Democrat,* on November 7, 1864.

> ARRIVED—The 14th regiment, numbering 530 men, rank and file, under command of Major Warren, arrived at this point on Saturday evening, to be mustered out of the service. This regiment has labored nobly in the field ever since it left home, and is entitled to great praise. We deem it a shame that a public reception had not been given these brave men who have thus stood the heat and burdens of the campaign. Surely they were entitled to have been warmly welcomed back to Iowa.

Apparently they were not.

---

158. Stuart, 275.

V. L. SPAWR,

DEALER IN

GROCERIES & PROVISIONS,

FRESH AND CURED MEATS,

HIDES,

POULTRY AND GAME.

NEOSHO FALLS, - - - - - - KANSAS.

Neosho Falls (Kansas) Post, April 19, 1876.

CHAPTER 9
AFTER THE WAR

Valentine Spawr, his wife and children, his parents, and his siblings moved to Neosho Falls, Kansas, in 1866. Spawr invested in real estate and owned a series of stores there, and he was made a trustee of the town when it was incorporated in 1870.

His sister Margaret ("Lou") Young said later in his widow's pension application affidavit that "at any time said Spawr would take cold or overexert himself he would take down with his lungs and be confined to his bed usually several weeks then would get better till he had another attack. He was confined to the house and bed and disabled from work at least one fourth of the time during which I was with him."

He moved his family to Gilman, Illinois, in 1876, and his wife died there in 1877. The 1880 census says he was a carpenter, but his neighbors later said in a pension application affidavit that he was unfit to perform manual labor because of his health. They said he had a bad cough and complained often about trouble with his lungs.

They said he never regained good health while they knew him.

In spite of his reported poor health, Spawr remarried in 1880. His new wife was Lusena Carley of Ashkum, Illinois. Spawr became father to her son Loren, and they had two children together, Clarence and Ruth. By 1882, they were in Kensington, a small railroad town south of Chicago that was booming because George M. Pullman had announced he was going to build the town of Pullman just north of it. Spawr probably moved there to find carpentry work; construction workers who worked on the new town lived in Kensington. He died there of pneumonia June 24, 1882, at about age 50. He is buried with his first wife in the Gilman Cemetery in Iroquois County.

His widow filed an application in 1883 for a pension based on lung disease he blamed on his service during the war. His Fourteenth Iowa friends Sergeant Myron Roberts and Captain Herman Miles were among those completing affidavits confirming his health was damaged during that time. "Soon after the return of my company from the battle of Pleasant Hill on Red River in Louisiana I noticed that he was troubled with a cough & he complained very much of his throat and lungs," Miles wrote.

Spawr's chaplain friend Frederick Kiner joined the Twenty-Seventh Iowa the January after the

Fourteenth was mustered out and served as chaplain for that regiment until the end of the war. He studied the law and was admitted to the bar in 1880. He died in the Iowa State Soldiers Home at age 67 in 1901.[159]

Colonel William T. Shaw returned to being a builder, developer, banker, and philanthropist in Anamosa, Iowa, and served in the state legislature in 1875–76. He wrote an article about Pleasant Hill for the State Historical Society of Iowa *Annals of Iowa* in 1898. He seemed to be trying one last time to set the record straight about the battle and the unfair odds he faced, but the article does not mention drunken officers, controversial letters, or his temporary dismissal. He died in 1909 at age 86.[160]

All but one of the Columbus recruits who did not desert and who survived the war remained in Company B of the Fourteenth's Residuary Battalion after the rest of the regiment was mustered out.[161]

The Fourteenth's flag was displayed at what was billed as the first reunion of the Fourteenth Iowa in October 1886. An article in the *Iowa State Register* ("Fourteenth Iowa Infantry: First Meet-

159. http://findagrave.com.

160. Shaw, "Battle at Pleasant Hill"; Corbitt, *History of Jones County, Vol. 2,* 11–12.

161. Thrift, *Roster and Record,* 731–879.

ing of the Regiment since the War," Des Moines, October 13, 1886) describes it as saying "Fourteenth Regiment Iowa Infantry Volunteers, Donelson, Shiloh, Corinth" and adds that those were the battles the regiment fought in before being taken prisoner in 1862. That is interesting because Spawr mentions only Donelson and Shiloh being on the flag in 1863. "It is very tender and considerably torn," the article says. It adds that it was carried into battle at Fort DeRussy, Pleasant Hill, Marksville, Old Oaks (Bayou des Glaises), Tupelo, and Old Town Creek. Pilot Knob is not mentioned but should have been. The Fourteenth's national and regimental flags are in storage at the State Historical Museum of Iowa in Des Moines.

Fort Halleck barely survived the war. The *New York Times* reported on June 2, 1865, "A portion of the bluff above Columbus, Ky., fell into the river to-day, carrying with it Fort Halleck and several buildings." The site is now the Columbus-Belmont State Park, where visitors can still see Civil War fortifications and one of the homes used as hospitals during the war. The anchor and part of the chain mentioned in Spawr's diary are on display there as well.[162]

---

162. Kentucky State Parks. "Columbus- Belmont," https://parks.ky.gov/parks/recreationparks/columbus-belmont/.

The earthwork walls of Fort Davidson in Pilot Knob, Missouri, still stand around the crater Ewing's troops left behind when they blew up the munitions and evacuated the fort.

APPENDIX

Roster of the Replacement Companies A–C, 14th Iowa, 1862–1865

Source: William Thrift, *Roster and Record of Iowa Soldiers in the War of the Rebellion. Vol. II, 9th–16th Regiments–Infantry.*

Company officers at the time of muster in do not have enlistment dates. Men who enlisted but were rejected by the mustering officer are not included.

Line Officers at Muster In

Company A

Isaac M. Talmage, Captain
Hugo Hoffbauer, First Lieutenant
William T. Dittoe, Second Lieutenant

Company B

Richard Currier, Captain
William V. Lucas, First Lieutenant
Andrew J. Allen, Second Lieutenant

Company C

______, Captain (no appointment on organization of company)
Herman A. Miles, First Lieutenant
William Stoughton, Second Lieutenant

Company A

Agans, John, 18. Residence LeClaire, born Michigan, Enlisted Aug. 21, 1862, as Fifer. Mustered Oct. 21, 1862. Mustered out Nov. 16, 1864, Davenport, Iowa.

Arenndo, Napoleon, 19. Residence Davenport, born Wisconsin. Enlisted Aug. 21, 1862. Mustered Oct. 21, 1862. Mustered out Nov. 16, 1864, Davenport, Iowa.

Bagley, George W., 18. Residence Davenport, born Iowa. Enlisted Feb. 9, 1863. Mustered Feb. 9, 1863. Mustered out Nov. 16, 1864, Davenport, Iowa.

Baldwin James, 23. Residence Davenport, born New York. Enlisted Aug. 21, 1862. Mustered Nov. 26, 1862. Promoted to wagoner. Wounded in forehead and died of wounds May 18, 1864, Old Oaks, La.

Banchman, Heinrich, 23. Residence Davenport, born Denmark. Enlisted Aug. 21, 1862. Mustered Nov. 26, 1862. Died of typhoid fever June 9, 1863, Cairo, Ill. Buried in National Cemetery, Mound City, Ill., Section B, grave 2256.

Bergheim, Charles, 26. Residence Davenport, born Prussia. Enlisted Jan. 17, 1863. Mustered Jan. 17, 1863. Deserted March 20, 1863, Davenport, Iowa.

Bergheim, Henry, 18. Residence Davenport, born Prussia. Enlisted Jan. 17, 1863. Mustered Jan. 17, 1863. Deserted March 20, 1863, Davenport, Iowa.

Bergheim, John, 21. Residence Davenport, born Prussia. Enlisted Jan. 17, 1863 Mustered Jan. 17, 1863. Deserted March 20, 1863, Davenport, Iowa.

Booth, Lyman, 18. Residence Davenport, born Michigan. Enlisted Dec. 23, 1862. Mustered Dec. 23, 1862. Mustered out Nov. 16, 1864, Davenport, Iowa.

Butler, Moses, 25. Residence Scott County, born New York. Enlisted Feb. 20, 1863. Mustered Feb. 20, 1863. Remained in Company A, Residuary Battalion.

Clarke, Joseph, 39. Residence Davenport, born Pennsylvania. Enlisted Aug. 21, 1862. Mustered Oct. 21, 1862. Mustered out November 1864, Davenport, Iowa.

Collins, Jesse H., 42. Residence Davenport, born Ohio. Enlisted Aug. 21, 1862. Mustered Oct. 21, 1862. Mustered out Nov. 16, 1864, Davenport, Iowa.

Dapron, Antonio, 21. Residence Davenport, born Wisconsin. Enlisted Aug. 21, 1862. Mustered Oct. 21, 1862. Mustered out Nov. 16, 1864, Davenport, Iowa.

Davenport, William A., 18. Residence Davenport, born Iowa. Enlisted Aug. 20, 1862. Mustered Oct. 21, 1862. Wounded in right ankle July 14, 1864, Tupelo, Miss. Died of wounds Aug. 6, 1864, Memphis, Tenn.

Dittoe, William T., 29. Residence Davenport, born Ohio. Enlisted Aug. 6, 1862, as First Sergeant. Mustered Oct. 21, 1862. Promoted Second Lieutenant Feb. 13, 1863. Mustered out Nov. 16, 1864, Davenport, Iowa.

Dorst, Conrad, 30. Residence Princeton, born Germany. Enlisted Aug. 20, 1862. Mustered Oct. 21, 1862. Mustered out Nov. 16, 1864, Davenport, Iowa.

Dougherty, Owen, 20. Residence Davenport, born Ireland. Enlisted Aug. 20, 1862. Mustered Oct. 21, 1862. Mustered out Nov. 16, 1864, Davenport, Iowa.

Drennan, Peter, 30. Residence Princeton, born Virginia. Enlisted Aug. 21, 1862 Mustered Oct. 21, 1862. Mustered out Nov. 16, 1864, Davenport, Iowa.

Farrell, Patrick, 19. Residence Davenport, born Ireland. Enlisted Aug. 16, 1862. Mustered Oct. 21, 1862. Deserted April 5, 1863, St. Louis, Mo.

Farrell, Timothy, 21. Residence Davenport, born Ireland. Enlisted Aug. 16, 1862. Mustered Oct. 21, 1862. Deserted April 5, 1863, St Louis, Mo.

Fechter, Cornelius, 24. Residence Davenport, born Germany. Enlisted March 11, 1863. Mustered March

25, 1863. Wounded in left shoulder July 15, 1864, near Tupelo, Miss. Mustered out Nov. 16, 1864, Davenport, Iowa.

Finley, Hiram, 21. Residence LeClaire, born Iowa. Enlisted Aug. 21, 1862. Mustered Oct. 21, 1862. Promoted Eighth Corporal Dec. 1, 1863; Seventh Corporal July 22, 1864. Mustered out Nov. 16, 1864, Davenport, Iowa.

Fitzgerald, Richard, 21. Residence Walnut Grove, born Ireland. Enlisted Aug. 21, 1862. Mustered Oct. 21, 1862. Wounded in left arm July 15, 1864, near Tupelo, Miss. Mustered out Nov. 16, 1864, Davenport, Iowa.

Frazier, William I., 28. Residence Davenport, born Pennsylvania. Enlisted Aug. 21, 1862. Mustered Oct. 21, 1862. Mustered out Nov. 16, 1864, Davenport, Iowa.

Gardner, Waldo P., 25. Residence LeClaire, born New York. Enlisted Aug. 21, 1862, as Second Sergeant. Mustered Oct. 21, 1862. Promoted First Sergeant Feb. 13, 1863. Mustered out Nov. 16, 1864, Davenport, Iowa.

Garity, Peter, 26. Residence Walnut Grove, born Ireland. Enlisted Aug. 21, 1862. Mustered Oct. 21, 1862. Deserted April 6, 1863, St. Louis, Mo.

Gorman, John B., 25. Residence Davenport, born France. Enlisted Aug. 1, 1862. Mustered Oct. 21, 1862.

Wounded in both legs April 9, 1864, Pleasant Hill, La. Mustered out Nov. 16, 1864, Davenport, Iowa.

Guion, William H. Jr, 19. Residence Davenport, born Ohio. Enlisted Aug. 21, 1862, as Second Corporal. Mustered Oct. 21, 1862. Promoted First Corporal Feb. 13, 1863. Reduced April 9, 1863. Promoted Eighth Corporal Sept. 27, 1863; Seventh Corporal Dec. 1, 1863; Sixth Corporal July 22, 1864. Mustered out Nov. 16, 1864, Davenport, Iowa. See Company B, Second Infantry.

Harvey, John, 20. Residence Blue Grass, born Missouri. Enlisted Aug. 21, 1862. Mustered Dec. 27, 1862. Discharged Nov. 14, 1864, Davenport, Iowa.

Harvey, William, 22. Residence Davenport, born Indiana. Enlisted Aug. 21, 1862. Mustered Oct. 21, 1862. Discharged for disability June 23, 1863.

Henry, Peter, 42. Residence Davenport, born Ireland. Enlisted Aug. 21, 1862. Mustered Oct. 21, 1862. Mustered out Nov. 16, 1864, Davenport, Iowa

Hire, John, 33. Residence Princeton, born Indiana. Enlisted Aug. 21, 1862 Mustered Oct. 21, 1862. Mustered out Nov. 16, 1864, Davenport, Iowa.

Hoffbauer, Hugo, 26. Residence Walcott, born Prussia. Appointed First Lieutenant Nov. 26, 1862. Mustered Nov. 26, 1862. Mustered out Nov. 16, 1864, Davenport, Iowa.

Hoffman, John, 21. Residence Walnut Grove, born Switzerland. Enlisted Aug. 21, 1862. Mustered Dec. 19, 1862. Mustered out Nov. 16, 1864, Davenport, Iowa.

Hyland, John, 23. Residence Walnut Grove, born Ireland. Enlisted Aug. 18, 1862. Mustered Oct. 21, 1862. Mustered out Nov. 16, 1864, Davenport, Iowa.

Jackson, James, 21. Residence Columbus, Ky., born Illinois. Enlisted Nov. 12, 1863. Mustered Nov. 14, 1863. Dropped. Turned back to the 119th Illinois Infantry (having left that regiment).

Kinkaid, Skiles W., 31. Residence Princeton, born Pennsylvania. Enlisted Aug. 21, 1862, as First Corporal. Mustered Oct. 21, 1862. Promoted Fifth Sergeant Feb. 13, 1863; Fourth Sergeant Dec. 1, 1863; Third Sergeant July 22, 1864. Mustered out Nov. 16, 1864, Davenport, Iowa.

Knapp, Jefferson W., 28. Residence Davenport, born Vermont. Enlisted Aug. 21, 1862. Mustered Oct. 21, 1862. Wounded in hand March 14, 1864, Fort DeRussy. Mustered out Nov. 16, 1864, Davenport, Iowa.

Lancaster, Benjamin P., 22. Residence LeClaire, born Illinois. Enlisted Aug. 21, 1862, as Sixth Corporal. Mustered Oct. 21, 1862. Promoted Fifth Corporal Feb. 13, 1863; Fourth Corporal April 1, 1863; Third

Corporal Dec. 1, 1863; Second Corporal July 22, 1864. Mustered out Nov. 16, 1864, Davenport, Iowa.

Lavender, Leonard, 32, Residence Walcott, born Ohio. Enlisted Aug. 21, 1862. Mustered Oct. 21, 1862. Promoted Eighth Corporal Feb. 13, 1863. Died of dysentery Sept. 11, 1863. Columbus, Ky. Buried in National Cemetery, Mound City, Ill., Section C, grave 3084.

Leacock, Samuel A., 26. Residence Davenport, born Pennsylvania. Enlisted Aug. 21, 1862, as Third Sergeant. Mustered Oct. 21, 1862. Promoted Second Sergeant Feb. 13, 1863. Deserted Dec. 1, 1863, Cairo, Ill.

Leslie, William M., 19. Residence Davenport, born Pennsylvania. Enlisted Aug. 21, 1862. Mustered Oct. 21, 1862. Mustered out Nov. 16, 1864, Davenport, Iowa.

Litscher, Bernhard, 18. Residence Walnut Grove, born Switzerland. Enlisted Oct. 21, 1862. Mustered Oct. 21, 1862. Mustered out Nov. 16, 1864, Davenport, Iowa.

Litscher, Christian, 21. Residence Walnut Grove, born Switzerland. Enlisted Aug. 21, 1862, as Eighth Corporal. Mustered Oct. 21, 1862. Promoted Seventh Corporal. Wounded in shoulder July 14, 1864, Tupelo, Miss. Mustered out Nov. 16, 1864, Davenport, Iowa.

Lynch, John, 25. Residence Davenport, born Ireland. Enlisted Aug. 20, 1862. Mustered Oct. 21, 1862. Mustered out Nov. 16, 1864, Davenport, Iowa.

McCloud, Samuel, 29. Residence Davenport, born Ireland. Enlisted Aug. 21, 1862. Mustered Oct. 21, 1862. Deserted March 29, 1863, Davenport, Iowa.

McIntyre, John, 27. Residence Davenport, born Pennsylvania. Enlisted Aug. 20, 1862. Mustered Oct. 21, 1862. Deserted April 5, 1863, St. Louis, Mo.

McKean, Francis, 21. Residence Davenport, born Ireland. Enlisted Aug. 21, 1862. Mustered Oct. 21, 1862. Wounded in left foot slightly April 9, 1864, Pleasant Hill, La. Mustered out Nov. 16, 1864, Davenport, Iowa.

McLoskey, Charles A., 18. Residence Davenport, born Iowa. Enlisted Aug. 15, 1863. Mustered Oct. 31, 1863. Mustered out Nov. 16, 1864, Davenport, Iowa.

McManus, Michael, 20. Residence Walnut Grove, born Indiana. Enlisted Aug. 21, 1862, as Third Corporal. Mustered Oct. 21, 1862. Promoted Second Corporal Feb. 13, 1863; First Corporal April 1, 1863; Fifth Sergeant Dec. 1, 1863; Fourth Sergeant July 22, 1864. Mustered out Nov. 16, 1864, Davenport, Iowa.

Miller, John C., 35. Residence Davenport, born Germany. Enlisted Aug. 20, 1862. Mustered Oct. 21, 1862. Missing and taken prisoner March 1, 1864. No further record.

Moore, Henry S., 23. Residence Davenport, born Massachusetts. Enlisted Aug. 21, 1862. Mustered Oct. 21, 1862. Died of lung fever Feb. 11, 1863, Davenport, Iowa.

Morrison, David, 39. Residence LeClaire, born Ireland. Enlisted Aug. 21, 1862. Mustered Oct. 21, 1862. Wounded in right hand April 9, 1864, Pleasant Hill, La. Mustered out Nov. 16, 1864, Davenport, Iowa.

Mower, Daniel, 28. Residence Davenport, born Pennsylvania. Enlisted Dec. 3, 1862. Mustered Dec. 3, 1862. Mustered out Nov. 16, 1864, Davenport, Iowa.

Nesbitt, Everett G., 28. Residence Davenport, born Pennsylvania. Enlisted Aug. 21, 1862. Mustered Oct. 21, 1862. Mustered out Nov. 16, 1864, Davenport, Iowa.

Pace, William H., 26. Residence Davenport, born Iowa. Enlisted Aug. 21, 1862. Mustered Oct. 21, 1862. Mustered out Nov. 16, 1864, Davenport, Iowa.

Palmer, David B., 34. Residence Princeton, born New York. Enlisted Aug. 21, 1862, as Fourth Sergeant. Mustered Oct. 21, 1862. Promoted Third Sergeant Feb. 13, 1863. Died of typhoid fever July 22, 1864, Memphis, Tenn. Buried in Mississippi River National Cemetery, Memphis, Tenn., Section 2, grave 326.

Paustian, Hans, 29. Residence Davenport, born Germany. Enlisted Aug. 21, 1862. Mustered Oct. 21, 1862. Died of fever Oct. 2, 1863, Columbus, Ky.

Pinneo, John, 15. Residence Princeton, born Iowa. Enlisted Jan. 8, 1863. Mustered Jan. 8, 1863. Promoted Fifer. Mustered out Nov. 16, 1864, Davenport, Iowa.

Pinneo, Mathias D., 42. Residence Princeton, born Vermont. Enlisted Aug. 21, 1862. Mustered Oct. 21, 1862. Died of fever May 19, 1864, Memphis, Tenn. Buried in Mississippi River National Cemetery, Memphis, Tenn., Section 2 grave 331.

Ramson, Benjamin, 35. Residence Davenport, born Ohio. Enlisted Aug. 21, 1862. Mustered Oct. 21, 1862. Discharged for disability Sept. 27, 1863, Columbus, Ky.

Reimas, Hans, 34. Residence Davenport, born Germany. Enlisted Aug. 21, 1862. Mustered Oct. 21, 1862. Promoted Eighth Corporal April 1, 1863; Seventh Corporal Sept. 27, 1863; Sixth Corporal Dec. 1, 1863; Fifth Corporal July 22, 1864. Mustered out Nov. 16, 1864, Davenport, Iowa.

Remington, Daniel, 28. Residence Davenport, born Ohio. Enlisted Aug. 21, 1862, as Fifth Sergeant. Mustered Oct. 21, 1862. Promoted Fourth Sergeant Feb. 13, 1863. Mustered out Nov. 16, 1864, Davenport, Iowa.

Robeson, Thomas M., 21. Residence Davenport, born Pennsylvania. Enlisted March 4, 1863. Mustered

March 4, 1863. Mustered out Nov. 16, 1864, Davenport, Iowa.

Roseman, Alfred, 18. Residence Blue Grass, born Ohio. Enlisted Aug. 21, 1862. Mustered Oct. 21, 1862. Discharged for disability Aug. 10, 1863.

Ruick, William F., 18. Residence Davenport, born Ohio. Enlisted Aug. 18, 1862. Mustered Oct. 14, 1862. Mustered out Nov. 16, 1864, Davenport, Iowa.

Russell, Daniel E., 27. Residence Walcott, born Ohio. Enlisted Aug. 21, 1862, as Fifth Corporal. Mustered Oct. 21, 1862. Promoted Fourth Corporal Feb. 13, 1863; Third Corporal April 1, 1863; Second Corporal Dec. 1, 1863; First Corporal, July 22, 1864. Mustered out Nov. 16, 1864, Davenport, Iowa.

Sank, John E., 44. Residence Princeton, born Maryland. Enlisted Aug. 21, 1862. Mustered Oct. 21, 1862. Mustered out Nov. 16, 1864, Davenport, Iowa.

Shabach, John, 42 Residence Buffalo, born Germany. Enlisted Aug. 21, 1862. Mustered Oct. 21, 1862. Mustered out Nov. 16, 1864, Davenport, Iowa.

Shlegle, Christian, 22. Residence Davenport, born Pennsylvania. Enlisted Dec. 1, 1862. Mustered Dec. 1, 1862. Mustered out Nov. 16, 1864, Davenport, Iowa.

Shmidt[*sic*], Peter D., 38. Residence Hickory Grove, born Germany. Enlisted Aug. 21, 1862. Mustered Oct. 21, 1862. Wounded in right shoulder March 14, 1864,

Fort DeRussy. Died of wounds May 13, 1864, Memphis, Tenn.

Shoemaker, Reuben B., 24. Residence Walnut Grove, born Pennsylvania. Enlisted Aug. 21, 1862. Mustered Oct. 26, 1862. Mustered out Nov. 16, 1864, Davenport, Iowa.

Sievers, Hans, 24. Residence Davenport, born Germany. Enlisted Aug. 20, 1862. Mustered Oct. 21, 1862. Discharged for disability July 12, 1864, St. Louis, Mo.

Slaughter, Fayette, 20. Residence Princeton, born New York. Enlisted Aug. 21, 1862. Mustered Oct. 21, 1862. Mustered out Nov. 16, 1864, Davenport, Iowa.

Sloper, David, 19. Residence LeClaire, born Iowa. Enlisted Aug. 21, 1862. Mustered Oct. 21, 1862. Promoted Seventh Corporal April 1, 1863; Sixth Corporal Sept. 27, 1863; Fifth Corporal Dec. 1, 1863. Wounded in left arm April 9, 1864, Pleasant Hill, La. Promoted Fourth Corporal July 22, 1864. Mustered out Nov. 16, 1864, Davenport, Iowa.

Smith, Charles C., 38. Residence Columbus, Ky., born Indiana. Enlisted Nov. 13, 1863. Mustered Nov. 14, 1863. Missing in action, April 9, 1864, Pleasant Hill, La. Deserted April 8, 1864, Grand Ecore, La.

Squyer, Horace D., 33. Residence Davenport, born New York. Enlisted Aug. 21, 1862, as wagoner. Mustered Oct. 21, 1862. Promoted Fourth Sergeant

April 13, 1863; Second Sergeant Dec. 1, 1863. Mustered out Nov. 16, 1864, Davenport, Iowa.

Stewart, William, 44. Residence Princeton, born Ireland. Enlisted Aug. 21, 1862. Mustered Oct. 21, 1862. Deserted March 29, 1863, Davenport, Iowa.

Sweeney, Charles, 33. Residence LeClaire, born Ireland. Enlisted Aug. 21, 1862. Mustered Oct. 30, 1862. Wounded in breast slightly April 9, 1864, Pleasant Hill, La. Mustered out Nov. 16, 1864, Davenport, Iowa.

Talmage, Isaac M., 25. Residence LeClaire, born New York. Appointed Captain Nov. 26, 1862. Mustered Nov. 26, 1862. Mustered out Nov. 16, 1864, Davenport, Iowa.

Turner, George, 41. Residence Davenport, born England. Enlisted Dec. 12, 1862. Mustered Dec. 12, 1862. Wounded in head April 9, 1864, Pleasant Hill, La. Wounded in thigh and arm July 14, 1864, Tupelo, Miss. Mustered out Nov. 16, 1864, Davenport, Iowa.

Vanduzer, James M., 21. Residence LeClaire, born Iowa. Enlisted Aug. 21, 1862, as Fourth Corporal. Mustered Oct. 21, 1862. Promoted Third Corporal Feb. 13, 1863; Second Corporal April 1, 1863; First Corporal Dec. 1, 1863. Wounded severely in right shoulder July 14, 1864, Tupelo, Miss. Promoted Fifth Sergeant July 22, 1864. Mustered out Nov. 16, 1864, Davenport, Iowa.

Veit, Jacob, 30. Residence Princeton, born Germany. Enlisted Aug. 21, 1862, as Seventh Corporal. Mustered Nov. 26, 1862. Promoted Sixth Corporal Feb. 13, 1863. Reduced to ranks at his own request Sept. 27, 1863. No further record.

Voglebach, John, 44. Residence Buffalo, born Germany. Enlisted Aug. 21, 1862. Mustered Oct. 21, 1862. Mustered out Nov. 16, 1864, Davenport, Iowa.

Voglebach, John C., 19. Residence Buffalo, born Ohio. Enlisted Jan. 12, 1862. Mustered Jan. 12, 1862. Mustered out Nov. 16, 1864, Davenport, Iowa.

White, Oliver, 23. Residence LeClaire, born Ohio. Enlisted Aug. 21, 1862, as drummer. Mustered Oct. 21, 1862. Mustered out Nov. 16, 1864, Davenport, Iowa.

Williams, Franklin, 28. Residence Princeton, born Arkansas. Enlisted Aug. 20, 1862. Mustered Oct. 21, 1862. Promoted Seventh Corporal Feb. 13, 1863; Fifth Corporal April 1, 1863; Fourth Corporal Dec. 1, 1863; Third Corporal July 22, 1864. Mustered out Nov. 16, 1864, Davenport, Iowa.

Williams, Samuel, 42. Residence Princeton, born Pennsylvania. Enlisted Aug. 21, 1862. Mustered Oct. 21, 1862. Promoted Eighth Corporal July 22, 1864. Mustered out Nov. 16, 1864, Davenport, Iowa.

Woolsey, Henry Clay, 19. Residence Davenport, born Illinois. Enlisted Jan. 3, 1863. Mustered Jan. 3, 1863. Mustered out Nov. 16, 1864, Davenport, Iowa.

Zink, George W., 22. Residence Bonaparte, born Missouri. Enlisted Oct. 2, 1861. Mustered Nov. 2, 1861. Transferred from Company F. Wounded in left leg April 9, 1864, Pleasant Hill, La. Mustered out Nov. 16, 1864, Davenport, Iowa. See Company F.

Zink, William, 18. Residence Bonaparte, born Iowa. Enlisted Jan. 28, 1863. Mustered Jan. 28, 1863. Mustered out Nov. 16, 1864, Davenport, Iowa.

Company B

Allen, Andrew J., 34. Residence Waverly, born New York. Enlisted Aug. 20, 1862, as First Sergeant. Mustered Nov. 26, 1862. Promoted Second Lieutenant Jan. 1, 1863; First Lieutenant April 11, 1863. Mustered out Nov. 16, 1864, Davenport, Iowa.

Arnel, James, 18. Residence Waverly, born Virginia. Enlisted Aug 20, 1862. Mustered Nov. 26, 1862. Mustered out Nov. 16, 1864, Davenport, Iowa.

Aurner, Hiram, 27. Residence Bremer County, born Michigan. Enlisted Aug. 20, 1862. Mustered Nov. 26, 1862. Killed in action April 9, 1864, Pleasant Hill, La.

Barclay, William H., 27. Residence Bremer County, born Pennsylvania. Enlisted Dec. 19, 1862. Mustered Feb. 14, 1863. Mustered out Nov. 16, 1864, Davenport, Iowa.

Baxley, George W., 30. Residence Sumner, born Virginia. Enlisted Aug. 20, 1862. Mustered Nov. 26, 1862. Deserted Dec. 31, 1863.

Becker, Charles, 26. Residence Waverly, born Prussia. Enlisted Aug. 18, 1862. Mustered Nov. 26, 1862. Deserted March 31, 1863, St. Louis, Mo.

Bevard, Darius, 19. Residence Bremer County, born Illinois. Enlisted Aug. 16, 1862. Mustered Nov. 26, 1862. Mustered out Nov. 16, 1864, Davenport, Iowa.

Bevard, James M., 18. Residence Bremer County, born Ohio. Enlisted Aug. 20, 1862. Mustered Nov. 26, 1862. Died of pneumonia Nov. 28, 1862, Camp Herron, Davenport, Iowa.

Bird, Charles, 22. Residence Bradford, born Illinois. Enlisted Aug. 22, 1862. Mustered Nov. 26, 1862. Mustered out Nov. 16, 1864, Davenport, Iowa.

Bisby, James, 41. Residence Fairview, born New York. Enlisted Oct. 18, 1862. Mustered Dec. 18, 1862. Discharged for disability March 27, 1863, Camp Herron, Davenport, Iowa.

Bodeker, August, 22. Residence Jefferson, born Germany. Enlisted Aug. 15, 1862. Mustered Nov. 26, 1862. Mustered out Nov. 16, 1864, Davenport, Iowa.

Boice, Thomas R., 29. Residence Jacksonville, born New York. Enlisted Aug. 18, 1862, as Seventh Corporal. Mustered Nov. 26, 1862. Promoted Sixth Corporal Jan. 1, 1863; Fifth Corporal April 11, 1863. Transferred to Invalid Corps June 1, 1864, Memphis, Tenn. Mustered out July 17, 1865, Rock Island, Ill.

Boyle, James, 23. Residence Monticello, born Ireland. Enlisted Dec. 17, 1862. Mustered Feb. 14, 1863. Mustered out Nov. 16, 1864, Davenport, Iowa.

Burge, William, 33. Residence Jefferson, born Ohio. Enlisted Aug. 9, 1862. Mustered Sept. 11, 1862. Transferred to Invalid Corps Sept. 1, 1863. No further record.

Campbell, George, 18. Residence Davenport, born Wisconsin. Enlisted Dec. 29, 1862. Mustered Dec. 29, 1862. Wounded severely April 9, 1864, Pleasant Hill, La. Mustered out June 25, 1865, Davenport, Iowa.

Carberry, Amos M., 22. Residence Jefferson, born Indiana. Enlisted Aug. 18, 1862. Mustered Sept. 11, 1862. Promoted Seventh Corporal July 1, 1864. Mustered out Nov. 16, 1864, Davenport, Iowa.

Chadwick, John J., 18. Residence Franklin, born Ohio. Enlisted Aug. 22, 1862. Mustered Sept. 11, 1862. Mustered out Nov. 16, 1864, Davenport, Iowa.

Churchill, Elias A., 35. Residence Tripoli, born Vermont. Enlisted Aug. 19, 1862. Mustered Sept. 11, 1862. Promoted Eighth Corporal April 11, 1863; Seventh Corporal Aug. 2, 1863; Fifth Corporal July 1, 1864. Mustered out Nov. 16, 1864, Davenport, Iowa.

Clark, Meroni, 20. Residence Jefferson, born Illinois. Enlisted Aug. 22, 1862. Mustered Sept. 11, 1862. Wounded and taken prisoner April 9, 1864. Pleasant Hill, La. Died of wounds July 15, 1864, Tyler, Texas.

Clarry, Jesse D., 18. Residence Washington, born Indiana. Enlisted Dec. 15, 1862. Mustered Dec. 15, 1862. Died of chronic diarrhoea July 19, 1864, Washington, Iowa.

Conner, Sanford E., 18. Residence Leroy, born New York. Enlisted Aug. 15, 1862. Mustered Sept. 11, 1862. Mustered out Nov. 16, 1864, Davenport, Iowa.

Currier, Richard, 37. Residence Waverly, born Massachusetts. Appointed Captain Nov. 26, 1862. Mustered Nov. 26, 1862. Resigned April 10, 1863.

Curttright, Thomas S., 24. Residence Davenport, born New York. Enlisted Aug. 15, 1862. Mustered Aug. 15, 1862. Deserted June 22, 1863, Cairo, Ill.

Dean, James W., 18. Residence Jefferson, born Illinois. Enlisted Aug. 12 1862. Mustered Sept. 11, 1862. Mustered out Nov. 16, 1864, Davenport, Iowa.

Dicken, Stephen M., 20. Residence Jefferson, born Illinois. Enlisted Aug. 17, 1862. Mustered Sept. 11, 1862. Wounded in right hand April 9, 1864, Pleasant Hill, La. Mustered out Nov. 16, 1864, Davenport, Iowa.

Dildine, William H., 36. Residence Jefferson, born New York. Enlisted Aug. 15, 1862. Mustered Sept. 11, 1862. Mustered out Nov. 16, 1864, Davenport, Iowa.

Dowd, David, 18. Residence Mount Pleasant, born Indiana. Enlisted Oct. 16, 1862. Mustered Nov. 5, 1862. Mustered out Nov. 16, 1864, Davenport, Iowa.

Dutcher, Albert W., 18. Residence Waverly, born Ohio. Enlisted Aug. 20, 1862. Mustered Nov. 26, 1862. Discharged June 26, 1863, Cairo, Ill.

Everstine, George L., 36. Residence Davenport, born Maryland. Enlisted Dec. 31, 1862. Mustered Dec. 31, 1862. Mustered out Nov. 16, 1864, Davenport, Iowa.

Farnsworth, Guy, 26. Residence Jefferson, born Pennsylvania Enlisted Aug. 22, 1862. Mustered Nov. 26, 1862. Mustered out Nov. 16, 1864, Davenport, Iowa.

George, William H., 25. Residence Fairfield, born Indiana. Enlisted Dec. 15, 1862. Mustered Dec. 15, 1862. Wounded slightly April 9, 1864, Pleasant Hill, La. Mustered out Nov. 16, 1864, Davenport, Iowa.

Gilmore, Joshua, 38. Residence Waverly, born Ohio. Enlisted Aug. 20, 1862, as Eighth Corporal. Mustered Sept. 11, 1862. Promoted Seventh Corporal Jan. 1, 1863; Sixth Corporal April 11, 1863. Died Aug. 2, 1863, Centralia, Ill.

Gors, Henry, 19. Residence Waverly, born Germany. Enlisted Aug. 22, 1862. Mustered Nov. 26, 1862. Died of pneumonia Dec. 1, 1862, Camp Herron, Davenport, Iowa. Buried in National Cemetery, Rock Island, Ill.

Graves, Cyrus B., 38. Residence Anamosa, born Vermont. Enlisted Oct. 12, 1862. Mustered Nov. 26, 1862. Died of chronic diarrhoea July 24, 1863, Columbus, Ky. Buried in National Cemetery, Mound City, Ill., Section C, grave 3084.

Greives, Robert, 44. Residence Waverly, born Scotland. Enlisted Aug. 22, 1862. Mustered Nov. 26, 1862. Mustered out Nov. 16, 1864, Davenport, Iowa.

Hall, Levi, 21. Residence Waverly, born Ohio. Enlisted Aug. 7, 1862. Mustered Nov. 26, 1862. Mustered out Nov. 16, 1864, Davenport, Iowa.

Harvey, Charles T., 38. Residence Anamosa, born Maryland. Enlisted Oct. 15, 1862. Mustered Nov. 26, 1862. Deserted Sept. 30, 1863, St. Louis, Mo.

Haun, George, 30. Residence Waverly, born Pennsylvania. Enlisted Aug. 20, 1862. Mustered Nov. 26, 1862. Promoted Eighth Corporal Aug. 30, 1863;

Sixth Corporal July 1, 1864. Mustered out Nov. 16, 1864, Davenport, Iowa.

Hawley, Levi P., 32. Residence Jacksonville, born Massachusetts. Enlisted Aug. 18, 1862. Mustered Nov. 26, 1862. Promoted Eighth Corporal July 1, 1864. Wounded in right side July 15, 1864, Tupelo, Miss. Mustered out Nov. 16, 1864, Davenport, Iowa.

Higgins, Hubert R., 19. Residence Jefferson, born New York. Enlisted Aug. 15, 1862. Mustered Nov. 26, 1862. Died of typhoid fever Aug. 18, 1863, Denver, Iowa.

Holden, John W., 24. Residence Anamosa, born Michigan. Enlisted Nov. 13, 1862. Mustered Nov. 13, 1862. Deserted March 27, 1863, Davenport Iowa.

Holmes, Allen E., 27. Residence Jefferson, born Ohio. Enlisted Aug. 15, 1862, as Second Sergeant. Mustered Nov. 26, 1862. Promoted First Sergeant Jan. 1, 1863; Second Lieutenant April 11, 1863. Wounded in left knee slightly April 9, 1864, Pleasant Hill, La. Mustered out Nov. 16, 1864, Davenport, Iowa.

Husband, Gasper T., 22. Residence Washington, born Pennsylvania. Enlisted Oct. 25, 1862. Mustered Nov. 26, 1862. Mustered out Nov. 16, 1864, Davenport, Iowa.

Keely, Thadeus, 31. Residence Jefferson, born Ohio. Enlisted Aug. 22, 1862, as Fifth Sergeant. Mustered Nov. 26, 1862. Promoted Fourth Sergeant Jan. 1,

1863; Third Sergeant April 11, 1863. Mustered out Nov. 16, 1864, Davenport, Iowa.

Kelly, John, 21. Residence Dubuque, born Tennessee. Enlisted Sept. 30, 1864. Mustered Oct. 6, 1864. Mustered out Nov. 16, 1864, Davenport, Iowa.

Kerr, John B., 20. Residence Franklin, born New York. Enlisted Aug. 15, 1862. Mustered Nov. 26, 1862. Wounded in left leg severely July 14, 1864, Tupelo, Miss. Mustered out Nov. 16, 1864, Davenport, Iowa.

Kimble, Francis W., 19. Residence Agency City, born Ohio. Enlisted Oct. 15, 1862, as drummer. Mustered Nov. 26, 1862. Mustered out Nov. 16, 1864, Davenport, Iowa.

Kingsbury, Winfield S., 18. Residence Mount Pleasant, born Indiana. Enlisted Dec. 14, 1862. Mustered Dec. 18, 1862. Wounded slightly in left side April 9, 1864, Pleasant Hill, La. Mustered out Nov. 16, 1864, Davenport, Iowa.

Krouse, John G., 18. Born Illinois. Enlisted Nov. 26, 1862. Mustered Dec. 18, 1862. Discharged Feb. 14, 1863, Davenport, Iowa.

Lamson, Earl J., 19. Residence Waverly, born New York. Enlisted Aug. 20, 1862, as Fourth Corporal. Mustered Nov. 26, 1862. Promoted Third Corporal Jan. 1, 1863; Second Corporal April 11, 1863; First Corporal July 1, 1864. Mustered out Nov. 16, 1864, Davenport, Iowa.

Legge, Frederick, 23. Residence Maxfield, born Germany. Enlisted Aug. 15, 1862. Mustered Nov. 26, 1862. Mustered out Nov. 16, 1864, Davenport, Iowa.

Leyle, Joseph R., 20. Residence Davenport, born Indiana. Enlisted Aug. 15, 1862. Mustered Nov. 26, 1862. Killed in action April 9, 1864, Pleasant Hill, La.

Littlefield, William C., 28. Residence Agency City, born Maine. Enlisted Oct. 17, 1862. Mustered Nov. 26, 1862. Mustered out Nov. 16, 1864, Davenport, Iowa.

Lucas, James A., 19. Residence Waverly, born Indiana. Enlisted Aug. 15, 1862. Mustered Nov. 26, 1862. Mustered out Nov. 16, 1864, Davenport, Iowa.

Lucas, William V., 27. Residence Waverly, born Ohio. Appointed First Lieutenant Nov. 26, 1862. Mustered Nov. 26, 1862. Promoted Captain April 11, 1863. Mustered out Nov. 16, 1864, Davenport, Iowa.

Mabb, William D., 25. Residence Sumner, born New York. Enlisted Aug. 20, 1862. Deserted previous to muster Sept. 11, 1862.

Meeker, Joshua, 24. Residence Denver, born Illinois. Enlisted Aug. 15, 1862. Mustered Sept. 11, 1862. Mustered out Nov. 16, 1864, Davenport, Iowa.

Meier, Henry, 21. Residence Maxfield, born Germany. Enlisted Dec. 23, 1863. Mustered Dec. 23, 1863. Taken prisoner April 9, 1864, Pleasant Hill, La. Remained in Company A, Residuary Battalion.

Messinger, John F. (1st), 31. Residence Jefferson, born Indiana. Enlisted Aug. 25, 1862. Mustered Nov. 26, 1862. Mustered out Nov. 16, 1864, Davenport, Iowa.

Messinger, John F. (2nd), 18. Residence Jefferson, born Iowa. Enlisted Nov. 26, 1862. Mustered Nov. 26, 1862. Died of congestion of brain Jan. 15, 1863, Davenport, Iowa.

Minard, Charles W., 18. Residence Monticello, born Illinois. Enlisted Dec. 17, 1862. Mustered Dec. 17, 1862. Mustered out Nov. 16, 1864, Davenport, Iowa.

Mohling, Christian, 21. Residence Jefferson, born Germany. Enlisted Aug. 15, 1862. Mustered Nov. 26, 1862. Mustered out Nov. 16, 1864, Davenport Iowa.

Moser, John, 37. Residence Franklin, born Switzerland. Enlisted Aug. 18, 1862. Mustered Nov. 26, 1862. Promoted Eighth Corporal Jan. 1, 1863; Seventh Corporal April 11, 1863; Sixth Corporal Aug. 2, 1863; Fourth Corporal July 1, 1864. Mustered out Nov. 16, 1864, Davenport, Iowa.

Murray, William B., 26. Residence Fairfield, born Virginia. Enlisted Sept. 4, 1862. Mustered Nov. 26, 1862. Discharged to accept promotion as Second Lieutenant of Company H, United States Colored Infantry, March 15, 1864, Helena, Ark.

Nergo, John, 27. Residence Maxfield, born Germany. Enlisted Dec. 11, 1863. Mustered Dec. 11, 1863. Taken prisoner Sept. 29, 1864, Pilot Knob, Mo. Remained in Company A, Residuary Battalion.

Nicol, Alexander F., 25. Residence Jefferson, born Michigan. Enlisted Aug. 15, 1862, as Third Corporal. Mustered Nov. 26, 1862. Promoted Second Corporal Jan. 1, 1863; Fifth Sergeant April 11, 1863. Wounded in left thigh slightly April 9, 1864, Pleasant Hill, La. Promoted Fourth Sergeant July 1, 1864. Mustered out Nov. 16, 1864, Davenport, Iowa.

O'Brien, Edward, 18. Residence Fremont, born Ireland. Enlisted Oct. 23, 1862. Mustered Nov. 26, 1862. Killed in action April 9, 1864, Pleasant Hill, La.

Parker, Sydney J., 21. Residence Franklin, born Ohio. Enlisted Aug. 22, 1862. Mustered Nov. 26, 1862. Killed in action April 9, 1864, Pleasant Hill, La.

Parmenter, William W., 25. Residence Waverly, born Vermont. Enlisted Aug. 20, 1862, as Third Sergeant. Mustered Nov. 26, 1862. Promoted Second Sergeant Jan. 1, 1863; First Sergeant April 11, 1863. Wounded in left shoulder dangerously April 9, 1864, Pleasant Hill, La. Mustered out Nov. 16, 1864, Davenport, Iowa.

Phillips, Sayles B., 18. Residence Waverly, born Rhode Island. Enlisted Aug. 15, 1862, as fifer. Mustered Nov. 26, 1862. Mustered out Nov. 16, 1864, Davenport, Iowa.

Rlchman, John, 23. Residence Maxfield, born Germany. Enlisted Aug. 15, 1862. Mustered Nov. 26, 1862. Mustered out Nov. 16, 1864, Davenport, Iowa.

Robinson, Alfred, 32. Residence Franklin, born Canada. Enlisted Aug. 22, 1862, as Second Corporal. Mustered Nov. 26, 1862. Promoted First Corporal Jan. 1, 1863; Fifth Sergeant July 1, 1864. Mustered out Nov. 16, 1864, Davenport, Iowa.

Rockwood, James B., 18. Residence Tripoli, born New York. Enlisted Oct 23, 1862. Mustered Nov. 26, 1862. Mustered out Nov. 16, 1864, Davenport, Iowa.

Runyon, Charles, 21. Residence Horton, born Michigan. Enlisted Aug. 15, 1862, as Sixth Corporal. Mustered Nov. 26, 1862. Promoted Fifth Corporal Jan. 1, 1863; Fourth Corporal April 11, 1863; Third Corporal July 1, 1864. Mustered out Nov. 16, 1864, Davenport, Iowa.

Scott, J. Lafayette, 25. Residence Davenport, born Ohio. Enlisted July 27, 1862, as First Corporal. Mustered Nov. 26, 1862. Promoted Fifth Sergeant Jan 1, 1863; Fourth Sergeant April 11, 1863. Died of typhoid fever June 13, 1864, New Orleans, La. Buried in National Cemetery, New Orleans, La.

Severine, John, 21. Residence Maxfield, born Germany. Enlisted Aug. 15, 1862. Mustered Nov. 26, 1862. Mustered out Nov. 16, 1864, Davenport, Iowa.

Shively, Samuel, 18. Residence Tripoli, born Illinois. Enlisted Oct. 23, 1862. Mustered Nov. 26, 1862. Mustered out Nov. 16, 1864, Davenport, Iowa.

Shoemaker, David W., 24. Residence Highland Grove, born Ohio. Enlisted Aug. 12, 1862, as wagoner. Mustered Nov. 26, 1862. Died of typhoid fever May 24, 1863, Cairo, Ill.

Shoemaker, Joseph, 21. Residence Dayton, born Germany. Enlisted Nov. 1, 1862. Mustered Nov. 26, 1862. Mustered out Nov. 16, 1864, Davenport, Iowa.

Sleeper, Stephen, 44. Residence Sumner, born New Hampshire. Enlisted Aug. 22, 1862. Mustered Nov. 26, 1862. Mustered out Nov. 16, 1864, Davenport, Iowa.

Smith, Elijah (veteran), 33. Residence Jefferson, born Illinois. Enlisted Aug. 15, 1862. Mustered Nov. 26, 1862. Transferred to Invalid Corps Sept. 1, 1863. Mustered out Jan. 3, 1865, Davenport, Iowa.

Sowers, John, 29. Residence Denver, born Pennsylvania. Enlisted Dec. 19, 1862. Mustered Dec. 19, 1862. Mustered out Nov. 16, 1864, Davenport, Iowa.

Thorp, Charles I., 40. Residence Sumner, born New York. Enlisted Aug. 22, 1862. Mustered Nov. 26, 1862. Died of gunshot wounds Sept. 27, 1864, Pilot Knob, Mo.

Tyler, Edwin H., 27. Residence Horton, born New York. Enlisted Aug. 22, 1862, as Fifth Corporal. Mustered Nov. 26, 1862. Promoted Fourth Corporal Jan. 1, 1863; Third Corporal April 11, 1863; Second Corporal July 1, 1864. Mustered out Nov. 18, 1864 [verified date].

Webb, Albert, 31. Residence Janesville, born Ohio. Enlisted Aug. 22, 1862. Mustered Nov. 26, 1862. Mustered out Nov. 16, 1864, Davenport, Iowa.

Wells, Harris G., 24. Residence Waverly, born Ohio. Enlisted Aug. 17, 1862, as Fourth Sergeant. Mustered Nov. 26, 1862. Promoted Third Sergeant Jan. 1, 1863; Second Sergeant April 11, 1863. Mustered out Nov. 16, 1864, Davenport, Iowa.

Westervelt, Lewis R., 20. Residence Jefferson, born Ohio. Enlisted Aug. 21, 1862. Mustered Nov. 26, 1862. Mustered out Nov. 16, 1862, Davenport, Iowa.

White, Thomas J., 18. Residence Mount Pleasant, born New York. Enlisted Dec. 14, 1862. Mustered Dec. 14, 1862. Discharged Feb. 16, 1863, Davenport, Iowa.

Wilkins, Henry, 18. Residence Millersburg, born New York. Enlisted Dec. 18, 1862. Mustered Feb. 14, 1863. Deserted April 11, 1863.

Willard, Curtis A., 22. Residence Anamosa, born Vermont. Enlisted Nov. 15, 1862. Mustered Nov. 15, 1862. Deserted March 27, 1863, Davenport, Iowa.

Winklepleck, Abraham, 24. Residence Jefferson, born Ohio. Enlisted Aug. 15, 1862. Mustered Nov. 26, 1862. Deserted Dec. 31, 1863.

Winklepleck, Noah, 21. Residence Jefferson, born Ohio. Enlisted Aug. 21, 1862. Mustered Nov. 26, 1862. Mustered out Nov. 16, 1864, Davenport, Iowa.

Winklepleck, Seth, 22. Residence Jefferson, born Ohio. Enlisted Aug. 15, 1862. Mustered Nov. 26, 1862. Mustered out Nov. 16, 1864, Davenport, Iowa.

Zoler, John, 18. Residence Dayton, born Germany. Enlisted Nov. 1, 1862. Mustered Nov. 26, 1862. Mustered out Nov. 16, 1864, Davenport, Iowa.

Company C

Ackroy, David, 32. Residence Columbus, born England. Enlisted Nov. 28, 1863. Mustered Dec. 11, 1863. Remained in Company B, Residuary Battalion.

Barrett, Andrew J., 35. Residence Davenport, born Ohio. Enlisted Dec. 11, 1862. Mustered May 2, 1863. Deserted Feb. 10, 1864, near Hillsboro, Miss.

Bartal, John, 18. Residence Cairo, Ill., born Illinois. Enlisted Dec. 1, 1863. Mustered Dec. 1, 1863. Taken prisoner Feb. 17, 1864, Meridian, Miss. Mustered out July 18, 1865, Davenport, Iowa.

Beckwith, Henry, 27. Residence Butler Center, born Canada. Enlisted Feb. 15, 1863. Mustered May 2, 1863. Promoted Second Sergeant May 23, 1863. Mustered out May 16, 1864, Davenport, Iowa.

Bird, Eli, 21. Residence Butler Center, born Canada. Enlisted Feb. 14, 1863. Mustered May 2, 1864. Mustered out Nov. 16, 1864, Davenport, Iowa.

Boylan, Cornelius, 18. Residence Clarksville, born Ohio. Enlisted Dec. 12, 1862. Mustered May 2, 1863. Taken prisoner Feb. 17, 1864, Meridian, Miss. Died in Andersonville Prison, Andersonville, Ga., Sept. 21, 1864. Buried in Andersonville National Cemetery, Andersonville, Ga., grave 9456.

Boylan, William H., 24. Residence West Point, born Indiana. Enlisted Nov. 1, 1862. Mustered May 2, 1863. Deserted Feb. 10, 1864, near Hillsboro, Mo.

Braden, John, 33. Residence Butler Center, born Ohio. Enlisted Nov. 1, 1862, as First Sergeant. Mustered May 2, 1863. Promoted First Lieutenant Dec. 21, 1863. Wounded Sept. 29, 1864, Leesburg, Mo. Died of wounds Oct. 31, 1864, Rollo, Mo.

Brown, Richard, 18. Residence Bremer County. Enlisted May 18, 1863. Mustered June 1, 1863. Mustered out Nov. 16, 1864, Davenport, Iowa.

Buckmaster, Fred C., 18. Residence Horton, born Ohio. Enlisted Oct. 16, 1862. Mustered May 2, 1863.

Taken prisoner Feb. 17, 1864, Meridian, Miss. Mustered out Nov. 16, 1864, Davenport, Iowa.

Burger, George, 18. Residence Butler County. Enlisted Feb. 24, 1863. Mustered May 2, 1863. Mustered out Nov. 16, 1864, Davenport, Iowa.

Chitester, Miles, 26. Residence Butler County, born Pennsylvania. Enlisted Feb. 14, 1863. Mustered May 2, 1863. Promoted Eighth Corporal Jan. 13, 1864; Sixth Corporal July 17, 1864. Mustered out Nov. 16, 1864, Davenport, Iowa.

Clarke, John, 40. Residence Columbus, Ky., born Ireland. Enlisted July 9, 1863. Mustered July 9, 1863. Promoted Eighth Corporal July 17, 1864. Remained in Company B, Residuary Battalion.

Coleman, Rufus C., 27. Residence Columbus, Ky., born Tennessee. Enlisted Nov. 28, 1863. Mustered Nov. 28, 1863. Discharged Jan. 26, 1864, Columbus, Ky.

Consadine, Henry P., 21. Residence Butler Center, born Nova Scotia. Enlisted Feb. 14, 1863, as Second Corporal. Mustered May 2, 1863. Promoted First Corporal May 23, 1863. Discharged March 15, 1864, Mound City, Ill.

Cook, Augustus A., 22. Residence Butler Center, born New York. Enlisted March 1, 1863. Mustered May 2, 1863. Promoted Fourth Corporal Dec. 28, 1863; Second Corporal Jan. 13, 1864; Fifth Sergeant July 17, 1864. Mustered out Nov. 16, 1864, Davenport, Iowa.

Cook, Hudson D., 28. Residence Butler Center, born New York. Enlisted March 1, 1863. Mustered May 2, 1863. Promoted Fifth Corporal May 23, 1863. Died of chronic diarrhoea while home on furlough Jan. 12, 1864.

Cotton, Theodore L., 18. Residence Shell Rock, born New York. Enlisted Nov. 1, 1862. Mustered May 2, 1863. Promoted Second Corporal May 23, 1863; First Corporal Jan. 13, 1864. Mustered out Nov. 16, 1864, Davenport, Iowa.

Couch, Manderville,18. Residence Butler County. Enlisted April 15, 1863. Mustered May 2, 1863. Mustered out Nov. 16, 1864, Davenport, Iowa.

Courtney, Lafayette, 21. Residence Columbus, Ky., born Kentucky. Enlisted Nov. 13, 1863. Mustered Nov. 13, 1863. Remained in Company B, Residuary Battalion.

Cummins, John R., 24. Residence Butler County. Enlisted Nov. 1, 1862. Mustered May 2, 1863. Wounded in action Sept. 27, 1864, Pilot Knob, Mo. Died of wounds Oct. 25, 1864, Cape Girardeau, Mo. Buried in National Cemetery, Jefferson Barracks, St. Louis, Mo., Section 50, grave 38.

Daniel, Charles T., 18. Born Tennessee. Enlisted Jan. 4, 1864. Mustered Jan. 4, 1864. Deserted Feb. 4, 1864, White River, Ark.

Davidson, Christopher P. 18. Residence Waterloo, born New York. Enlisted Nov. 6, 1862. Mustered May 2, 1863. Died of typhoid fever Sept. 6, 1863, Columbus, Ky.

Davidson, Thomas L., 23. Residence Bremer County. Enlisted Nov. 1, 1862. Mustered May 2, 1863. Wounded May 18, 1864, Bayou de Glaize, La. Mustered out Nov. 16, 1864, Davenport, Iowa.

Dawson, Martin, 22. Residence Butler County. Enlisted April 15, 1863. Mustered May 2, 1863. Transferred to Invalid Corps Nov. 29, 1864, Davenport, Iowa. Mustered out Nov. 16, 1864, Davenport, Iowa.

Dexter, Charles A., 36. Residence Dubuque, born Connecticut. Enlisted Jan. 10, 1863. Mustered May 2, 1863. Discharged for disability March 19, 1864, Mound City, Ill.

Dodson, Jones M., 23. Residence Columbus, Ky., born Kentucky. Enlisted Dec. 3, 1863. Mustered Dec. 3, 1863. Remained in Company B, Residuary Battalion.

Dyer, William C., 18. Born Tennessee. Enlisted Jan. 4, 1864. Mustered Jan. 4, 1864. Deserted Feb. 4, 1864, White River, Ark.

Fisher, Irving M., 25. Residence Nashua, born Massachusetts. Enlisted Oct. 12, 1862. Mustered May 2, 1863. Promoted Fourth Sergeant May 23, 1863;

Third Sergeant July 17, 1864. Mustered out Nov. 16, 1864, Davenport, Iowa.

Fisk, Andrew J., 19. Residence Columbus, Ky., born Kentucky. Enlisted Dec. 3, 1863. Mustered Dec. 3. 1863. Died of chronic diarrhoea Feb. 23, 1864, Decatur, Miss.

Fulgham, James J., 27. Residence Columbus, Ky., born Tennessee. Enlisted Sept. 28, 1863. Mustered Oct. 24, 1863. Deserted Jan. 23, 1864, Columbus, Ky.

Gambell, John H., 33. Residence Columbus, Ky., born Kentucky. Enlisted Dec. 3, 1863. Mustered Dec. 3, 1863. Killed in action April 9, 1864, Pleasant Hill, La.

Gipson, William J., 28. Residence Columbus, Ky., born Kentucky. Enlisted Oct. 15, 1863. Mustered Oct. 24, 1863. Deserted April 8, 1864, Grand Ecore, La.

Goforth, Thomas J., 19. Residence Columbus, Ky., born Kentucky. Enlisted Dec. 22, 1863. Mustered Dec. 22, 1863. Deserted July 29, 1864, Memphis, Tenn.

Halstead, William R., 19. Residence Butler County. Enlisted May 12, 1863. Mustered June 1, 1863. Died of chronic diarrhoea July 8, 1864, Memphis, Tenn.

Harlan, Joseph D., 28. Residence Columbus, Ky., born Kentucky. Enlisted Oct. 14, 1863. Mustered Oct. 24, 1863. Remained in Company B, Residuary Battalion.

Harman, Abner, 18. Residence Bremer County, born New York. Enlisted March 1, 1863. Mustered May 2, 1863. Promoted Fifth Corporal Jan. 13, 1864; Fourth Corporal July 17, 1864. Mustered out Nov. 16, 1864, Davenport, Iowa.

Inman, Frank E., 20. Residence Butler Center, born Illinois. Enlisted Nov. 1, 1862. Mustered May 2, 1863. Promoted Fourth Corporal May 20. 1863. Died of chronic diarrhoea June 24, 1864. Memphis, Tenn. See Company I, Ninth Infantry.

Johnson, Isaac T., 21. Born Kentucky. Enlisted Jan. 5, 1864. Mustered Jan. 5, 1864. Remained in Company B, Residuary Battalion.

Johnson, Jacob H., 36. Residence Columbus, Ky., born Kentucky. Enlisted Dec. 2, 1863. Mustered Dec. 2, 1863. Deserted Jan. 23, 1864.

Johnson, John H., 23. Residence Hickman, born Kentucky. Enlisted Jan. 6, 1864. Mustered Jan. 5, 1864. Died of chronic diarrhoea Nov. 10, 1864, Davenport, Iowa.

Keith, Roswell, 40. Residence Waverly, born New York. Enlisted Oct. 9, 1862, as First Corporal. Mustered May 2, 1863. Promoted Third Sergeant May 23. 1863, Died while home on furlough July 16, 1864, Waverly, Iowa.

Kidd, William, 18. Born Kentucky. Enlisted Jan. 4, 1864. Mustered Jan. 4, 1864. Deserted Feb. 4, 1864, near White River, Ark.

Lashbrook, Royal,18. Residence Bremer County. Enlisted Oct. 16, 1862. Mustered May 2, 1863. Mustered out Nov. 16, 1864, Davenport, Iowa.

Linahan William L36, born Ireland Enlisted Dec 1 1863 Mustered Dec 11 1863 Remained in Company B, Residuary Battalion.

Luckey, James R.,18. Residence Louisa County. Enlisted Jan. 8, 1863. Mustered May 2, 1863. Mustered out Nov. 16, 1864, Davenport, Iowa.

Lunsford, Aris Riley,19. Born Tennessee. Enlisted Jan. 4, 1864. Mustered Jan. 4, 1864. Deserted Feb. 5, 1864, near Jeff Davis Plantation, Mississippi.

Lynhern, William, 32. Residence Columbus, Ky., born Ireland. Enlisted July 9, 1863. Mustered July 9, 1863. Mustered out Nov. 16, 1864, Davenport, Iowa.

McAllaster, Asahel P., 18. Residence Shell Rock, born Illinois. Enlisted May 16. 1863, Mustered June 1, 1863. Taken prisoner Feb. 10, 1864, Meridian, Miss. Died in Andersonville prison June 16, 1864. Buried in National Cemetery, Andersonville, Ga., grave 2027.

McGinley, William, 44. Residence Dubuque, born Ireland. Enlisted Jan. 10, 1863. Mustered May 2, 1863. Died of chronic diarrhoea Jan. 24, 1864,

Columbus, Ky. Buried in National Cemetery, Mound City, Ill., Section C, grave 3079.

Margretz, John H., 19. Residence Butler Center, born Pennsylvania. Enlisted Nov. 1, 1862. Mustered May 2, 1863. Promoted Fourth Corporal Jan. 13, 1864; Third Corporal July 17, 1864. Mustered out Nov. 16, 1864, Davenport, Iowa.

Mathews, Anthony, 23. Residence Cass County, Indiana, born Indiana. Enlisted Aug. 30, 1863. Mustered Aug. 30, 1863. Deserted March 29, 1864, Vicksburg, Miss.

Maywood, John, 38. Residence Scott County. Enlisted April 28, 1863. Mustered May 2, 1863. Mustered out Nov. 16, 1864, Davenport, Iowa.

Miles, Herman A., 37. Residence Waverly, born Vermont. Appointed First Lieutenant May 2, 1863. Mustered May 2, 1863. Promoted Captain Dec. 21, 1863. Mustered out Nov. 16, 1864, Davenport, Iowa.

Misson, Alexander, 39. Residence Cairo, Ill., born West India Island. Enlisted Dec. 1, 1863. Mustered Dec. 1, 1863. Deserted June 24, 1864, Memphis, Tenn.

Morgan, William, 16. Residence Waverly, born Illinois. Enlisted May 15, 1863, as drummer. Mustered June 1, 1863. Deserted Sept. 28, 1863, Columbus, Ky.

Mowfield, William, 18. Residence Columbus, Ky., born Kentucky. Enlisted Dec. 3, 1863. Mustered Dec. 11,

1863. Taken prisoner Sept. 27, 1864, Pilot Knob, Mo. Remained in Company B, Residuary Battalion.

Myers, John, 35. Residence Columbus, Ky., born North Carolina. Enlisted Dec. 2, 1863. Mustered Dec. 11, 1863. Wounded in back slightly April 8, 1864, Pleasant Hill, La. Remained in Company B, Residuary Battalion.

Myers, Uriah, 21. Residence Butler County. Enlisted Feb. 15, 1863. Mustered May 2, 1863. Mustered out Nov. 16, 1864, Davenport, Iowa.

Oakes, Jesse, 18. Residence Columbus, Ky., born Kentucky. Enlisted Dec. 8, 1863. Mustered Dec. 11, 1863. Deserted Feb. 25, 1864, near Hillsboro Miss.

Outcult, Frederick, 43. Residence Black Hawk County. Enlisted May 7, 1863. Mustered June 1, 1863. Mustered out Nov. 16, 1864, Davenport, Iowa. See Company H, Eighth Cavalry, and Company A, Thirty-seventh Infantry.

Parsons, Joshua, 18. Residence Floyd County. Enlisted May 11, 1863. Mustered June 1, 1863. Mustered out Nov. 16, 1864, Davenport, Iowa.

Phipps, James S., 18. Residence Columbus, born Tennessee. Enlisted Nov. 28, 1863. Mustered Dec. 23, 1863. Died of chronic diarrhoea May 18, 1864, Alexandria, La.

Pickett, David C., 18. Residence Millburn, Ky., born Kentucky. Enlisted Oct. 27, 1863. Mustered Oct. 28, 1863. Remained in Company B, Residuary Battalion.

Pickett, Jasper, 18. Residence Columbus, born Tennessee. Enlisted Dec. 7, 1863. Mustered Dec. 11, 1863. Deserted Feb. 10, 1864, Hillsboro, Miss.

Pinkerton, Marion, 28. Residence Columbus Ky., born Tennessee. Enlisted Nov. 5, 1863. Mustered Nov. 5, 1863. Died of smallpox April 19, 1864, Memphis, Tenn. Buried in Mississippi River National Cemetery, Memphis, Tenn., Section 1, grave 22.

Proctor, Calvin R., 25. Residence Columbus, born Kentucky. Enlisted Nov. 30, 1863. Mustered Nov. 30, 1863. Remained in Company B, Residuary Battalion.

Pulley, Jesse, 18. Residence Columbus, born Tennessee. Enlisted Dec. 3, 186.3 Mustered Dec. 11, 1863. Remained in Company B, Residuary Battalion.

Robbins, Barney W., 18. Residence Waverly, born Pennsylvania. Enlisted Dec. 2, 1862. Mustered May 2, 1862. Promoted Sixth Corporal May 23, 1863. Died of pneumonia in hospital Nov. 1, 1863, Columbus, Ky. Buried in National Cemetery, Mound City, Ill., Section C, grave 3059.

Roberts, Myron L., 26. Residence Delaware, born New York. Enlisted Nov. 3, 1862. Mustered May 2, 1863. Promoted Fifth Sergeant May 23, 1863. Wounded and taken prisoner April 9, 1864, Pleasant Hill, La.

Promoted Fourth Sergeant July 17, 1864. Mustered out Nov. 16, 1864, Davenport, Iowa.

Scott, John, 28. Residence Columbus, born Missouri. Enlisted Dec. 2, 1863. Mustered Dec. 2, 1863. Deserted Feb. 6, 1864, near Jeff Davis Plantation, Mississippi.

Seaman, William L., 36. Residence Columbus Ky., born New York. Enlisted Dec. 1, 1863. Mustered Dec. 1, 1863. Deserted Sept. 8, 1864, Cairo, Ill.

Sherard, Benjamin W., 42. Residence Cairo, Ill., born North Carolina. Enlisted Dec. 1, 1863. Mustered Dec. 1, 1863. Deserted Oct. 22, 1864, St. Louis, Mo.

Slankard, John W., 27. Residence Hickman Ky., born Illinois. Enlisted Nov. 2, 1863. Mustered Nov. 9, 1863. Promoted Third Corporal Jan. 13, 1864; Second Corporal July 17, 1864. Deserted Sept. 8, 1864, Columbus, Ky.

Smith, Franklin S., 22. Residence Fayette, born Pennsylvania. Enlisted March 6, 1863. Mustered May 2, 1863. Promoted wagoner June 25, 1863. Mustered out Nov. 16, 1864, Davenport, Iowa.

Spawr, Valentine L., 28. Residence Clarksville, born Illinois. Enlisted Oct. 20, 1862. Mustered May 2, 1863. Promoted Eighth Corporal May 20, 1863; First Sergeant May 1, 1864. Mustered out Nov. 16, 1864, Davenport, Iowa.

Stoughton, William, 32. Residence Shell Rock, born Vermont. Appointed Second Lieutenant May 2, 1863. Mustered May 2, 1863. Resigned Jan. 23, 1864.

Streeter, Henry W., 18. Residence Waverly, born New York. Enlisted May 15, 1863. Mustered June 1, 1863. Deserted Feb. 27, 1864, near Pearl River, Miss.

Stuart, Charles, 18. Residence Butler County, born Canada. Enlisted Dec. 22, 1863. Mustered Dec. 22, 1863. Remained in Company B, Residuary Battalion.

Tenaure, Charles H., 18. Residence Horton, born Pennsylvania. Enlisted Oct. 16, 1862. Mustered May 2, 1863. Discharged for disability Dec. 4, 1863, Columbus, Ky.

Todd, Joseph M., 18. Born Kentucky. Enlisted Jan. 5, 1864. Mustered Jan. 5, 1864. Deserted Feb. 10, 1864. near Hillsboro, Miss.

Trofford, William J., 18. Residence Columbus, Ky., born Kentucky. Enlisted Nov. 8, 1863. Mustered Nov. 8, 1863. Deserted Feb. 25, 1864, near Hillsboro, Miss.

Tucker, Lewis, 18. Residence Fredonia, born Iowa. Enlisted April 20, 1863. Mustered May 2, 1863. Died of congestive chills Jan. 5, 1864, Columbus, Ky.

Van Dyke, Jacob D. W., 18. Residence Louisa County. Enlisted Oct. 14, 1862. Mustered May 2, 1863. Mustered out Nov. 16, 1864, Davenport, Iowa.

Wade, John, 38. Residence Philadelphia, Pa., born Ireland. Enlisted June 16, 1863. Mustered June 16, 1863. Remained in Company B, Residuary Battalion.

Wait, William H., 18. Residence Charles City, born Canada. Enlisted Oct. 20, 1862. Mustered May 2, 1863. Promoted Third Corporal May 23, 1863. Died of chronic diarrhoea May 9, 1864, Charles City, Iowa, while home on furlough.

Walling, James P., 18. Residence Bremer County. Enlisted Oct. 13, 1862. Mustered May 2, 1863. Mustered out Nov. 16, 1864, Davenport, Iowa.

Washburn, Scott, 18. Residence Muscatine County. Enlisted Feb. 20, 1863. Mustered May 2, 1863. Mustered out Nov. 16, 1864, Davenport, Iowa.

Watson, Edmond, 25. Residence Columbus, Ky., born Kentucky. Enlisted Oct. 14, 1863. Mustered Oct. 24, 1863. Remained in Company B, Residuary Battalion.

Watson, James, 27. Residence Columbus Ky., born Kentucky. Enlisted Dec. 4, 1863. Mustered Dec. 4, 1863. Deserted Sept. 8, 1864, Columbus, Ky.

Weber, Morman, 29. Residence Chickasaw County. Enlisted Oct. 18, 1862. Mustered May 2, 1863. Mustered out Nov. 16, 1864, Davenport, Iowa.

Wells, Ward S., 44. Residence Chickasaw County. Enlisted Oct. 18, 1862. Mustered May 2, 1863. Died of typhoid fever May 15, 1864, Memphis, Tenn. Buried in

Mississippi River National Cemetery, Memphis, Tenn., Section 1, grave 281.

Wetsel James T32 Residence Butler County Enlisted Dec 15 1862 Mustered May 2, 1863. Mustered out Nov. 16, 1864, Davenport, Iowa.

Wetsel, Thomas C., 18. Residence Butler County. Enlisted Feb. 20, 1863. Mustered May 2, 1863. Promoted Sixth Corporal Jan. 13, 1864; Fifth Corporal July 17, 1864. Mustered out Nov. 16, 1864, Davenport, Iowa.

Whitcomb, Marcellus, 32. Residence Delaware, born New York. Enlisted April 15, 1863. Mustered May 2, 1863. Promoted Seventh Corporal May 23, 1863. Mustered out Nov. 16, 1864, Davenport, Iowa.

Winchell, Lyford H., 18. Residence Shell Rock, born Indiana. Enlisted Oct. 28, 1862. Mustered May 2, 1863. Died of chronic diarrhoea Nov. 12, 1863, Shell Rock, Iowa.

Wright, Philander D., 18. Residence Bremer County. Enlisted Nov. 1, 1863. Mustered Nov, 1, 1863. Mustered out Nov. 16, 1864, Davenport, Iowa.

BIBLIOGRAPHY

Benson, S. F. "The Battle of Pleasant Hill, Lousiana." *Annals of Iowa* 7, no. 7 (1906): 481–504. http://doi.org/ 10.17077/0003-4827.3321

"Ben Van Dyke's Escape from the Hospital at Pleasant Hill, Louisiana." *Annals of Iowa* 7 (1906), 523–532. Ben Van Dyke's narrative, edited by Solomon Benson. https://doi.org/10.17077/0003-4827.3324

Byers, Samuel Hawkins Marshall. *Iowa in War Times.* Des Moines: W. D. Condit & Company, 1888. https://books.google.com/books?id=kYkNFuHHvx0C

Corbit, Robert. *History of Jones County, Iowa: Past and Present.* Chicago: S. J. Clarke Publishing Co., 1910. https://books.google.com/books?id=QYEUAAAAYAAJ

Donnan, William G. "A Reminiscence of the Last Battle of the Red River Expedition." *Annals of Iowa* 6 (1904), 241–247. https://doi.org/10.17077/0003-4827.2969

Elkins, Stephen B., comp. Chapter 51, "Operations in Kentucky, Southwest Virginia, Tennessee, Mississippi, Alabama, and North Georgia (The Atlanta Campaign Excepted): May 1–November 13, 1864." In *The War of the Rebellion: A Compilation of the Official Records of the Union and Confederate Armies.* Series I, Vol. 39, Part I, Reports. Washington, Government Printing

Office, 1892.
https://books.google.com/books?id=ecFZAAAAYAAJ

Ewing, Thomas Jr. "Battles of Pilot Knob and Leesburg, Missouri: General Ewing's Official Report." In *Fourteen Portraits on Steel, and Various Maps and Diagram.* Vol. 11 of *The Rebellion Record: A Diary of American Events, with Documents, Narratives, Illustrative Incidents, Poetry, Etc.,* edited by Frank Moore. New York: D. Van Nostrand, 1868.
https://books.google.com/books?id=qLQTAAAAYAAJ

Heath, William H. "Battle of Pleasant Hill Louisiana." *Annals of Iowa* 7 (1906), 516–522.
https://doi.org/10.17077/0003-4827.3323

Ingersoll, Lurton Dunham. *Iowa and the Rebellion: A History of the Troops Furnished by the State of Iowa to the Volunteer Armies of the Union, which Conquered the Great Southern Rebellion of 1861-5.* Philadelphia: J. B. Lippincott, 1866.
https://books.google.com/books?id=oVs7AQAAMAAJ

Johnson, Robert Underwood, and Clarence Clough Buel, eds. "The Defense of the Red River" in *Battles and Leaders of the Civil War.* Vol. 4, *Being for the Most Part Contributions by Union and Confederate Officers.* New York: Century Company, 1884, 1888.
https://books.google.com/books?id=yhhPAQAAMAAJ

Otis, George A., comp. "Chronological Summary: Engagements and Battles." In Surgical History, XXXIV–CLV (34–155, Roman numerals used for page numbers). Part 1, Vol. 2 of *Medical and Surgical History of the War of the Rebellion (1861–65),* compiled by

Joseph K. Barnes. Washington, Government Printing Office, 1870. https://books.google.com/books?id=kjVFAAAAcAAJ

Peterson, Cyrus Asbury, and Joseph Mills Hanson. *Pilot Knob: The Thermopylae of the West.* New York: Neale Publishing Company, 1914. https://books.google.com/books?id=XG65fxYYwV8C

Proctor, Redfield, comp. *The War of the Rebellion: A Compilation of the Official Records of the Union and Confederate Armies.* Series I, Vol. 38, Part V, Correspondence, Etc. Washington Government Printing Office, 1891. https://books.google.com/books?id=yvF2AAAAMAAJ

"Reports of Battles, Skirmishes, Etc., and Histories of Regiments," Appendix K in *Report of the Adjutant General and Acting Quartermaster General of the State, January 11, 1864, to January 1, 1865,* 931–1132. Des Moines, Iowa: F. W. Palmer, state printer, 1865. https://books.google.com/books?id=W_w_AAAAYAAJ

"Reports of Battles, Skirmishes, Etc., and Histories of Regiments," Appendix E in *Report of the Adjutant General and Acting Quartermaster General of the State, Jan. 1, 1865, to Jan. 1, 1866,* 108–446. Des Moines, Iowa: F. W. Palmer, state printer, 1866. https://books.google.com/books?id=bdY1AQAAMAAJ

Scott, Robert N., comp. "February 3–March 6, 1864—The Meridian, Miss., Expedition, and Cooperating Expeditions from Memphis, Tenn., and up the Yazoo River," 164–391. In "Operations in Kentucky, Southwest Virginia, Tennessee, Mississippi, Alabama, and North Georgia, January 1–April 30, 1864." Chapter 44 in Part 1, "Reports," of Series 1, Vol. 32 of *The War of the Rebellion: A Compilation of the Official Records of the Union and Confederate Armies*. Washington: Government Printing Office, 1891. https://books.google.com/books?id=MpItAAAAIAAJ

Scott, Robert N., comp. "Operations in Louisiana and the Trans-Mississippi States and Territories, January 1–June 30, 1864." Chapter 46 in Part 1, "Reports," of Series 1, Vol. 34 of *The War of the Rebellion: A Compilation of the Official Records of the Union and Confederate Armies*. Washington: U.S. Government Printing Office, 1891. https://books.google.com/books?id=Yb1ZAAAAYAAJ

Shambaugh, Benjamin F., ed. *Proceedings of the Mississippi Valley Historical Association for the Year 1908–1909*, Volumes 2-3. Cedar Rapids, IA: Torch Press, 1910. https://books.google.com/books?id=XElIAAAAYAAJ

Shaw, William T. Letter report March 17, 1864, in "Brigade, Division, Corps, and Miscellaneous Reports," in Appendix K, "Reports of Battles, Skirmishes, Etc., and Histories of Regiments," in *Report of the Adjutant General and Acting Quartermaster General of the State, January 11, 1864, to January 1, 1865*. Des Moines, Iowa: F. W. Palmer, state printer, 1865. https://books.google.com/books?id=W_w_AAAAYAAJ

Shaw, William T. "The Battle of Pleasant Hill." *Annals of Iowa* 3 (1898), 401–423. http://doi.org/10.17077/0003-4827.2332

Stuart, Addison A. *Iowa Colonels and Regiments: Being a History of Iowa Regiments in the War of the Rebellion; and Containing a Description of the Battles in which They Have Fought.* Mills & Company, 1865 – Iowa. https://books.google.com/books?id=G5cvAAAAYAAJ

Thrift, William H., ed. "New Enlistment" in *Roster and Record of Iowa Soldiers in the War of the Rebellion: 9th–16th Regiments–Infantry.* Vol. 2 of *Roster and Record of Iowa Soldiers in the War of the Rebellion: Together with Historical Sketches of Volunteer Organizations, 1861–1866.* Des Moines: E. H. English, Iowa State Printer, 1908. 755–781. https://books.google.com/books?id=TkMuAAAAYAAJ

War Department. Vol. 2, *1864-1865, Issues 14-52.* In *Army & Navy Official Gazette: Containing Reports of Battles; Also, Important Orders of the War Department, Records of Courts-Martial, Etc.* Washington City: 1865. https://books.google.com/books?id=ePkVZ9RSsacC

INDEX

M

N

O

P

Q

R

Made in the USA
Columbia, SC
20 March 2025

55424073R00198